MIRACLES ON THE BORDER

MIRACLES ON THE BORDER

Retablos of Mexican Migrants
to the United States

Jorge Durand & Douglas S. Massey

With Photographs by the Authors

The University of Arizona Press

Tucson and London

99 98 97 96 95   5 4 3 2 1

Library of Congress Cataloging-in-Publication Data

Durand, Jorge.

Miracles on the border : retablos of Mexican migrants to
the United States / Jorge Durand & Douglas S. Massey ; with
photographs by the authors.

p.   cm.

Includes bibliographical references (p.   –   ) and index.

ISBN 0-8165-1471-2 (cl : acid-free paper). —

ISBN 0-8165-1497-6 (pb : acid-free paper)

1. Painting, Mexican.   2. Christian art and symbolism—Modern
period, 1500–   —Mexico.   3. Votive offerings in art—Mexico.
4. Folk art—Mexico.   I. Massey, Douglas S.   II. Title.

ND1432.M46D87   1995   94-32080

755′.2—dc20   CIP

British Cataloguing-in-Publication Data

A catalogue record for this book is available from the British Library.

For Sol and Vanessa,

who without knowing much about art or religion

can appreciate this expression of

popular Mexican culture

▼

Contents
▼▼▼

Illustrations

Map

Tables
▼▼▼

Foreword
▼▼▼

This book is truly unique not only in its content, of course, but also in the authors who have produced it. It presents in narrative form the odyssey of Mexicans who have been obliged to emigrate to the United States in search of work. There is ample bibliography on this topic; however, the originality of this work lies in its presentation of history as told by the migrants themselves (and their families), also in the form through which they have chosen to tell it—an old and deep-seated expression of Mexican popular religiosity: the retablo.

The retablo expresses in picture form the adventures lived by the protagonist, and within each picture he also tells his story in words in a comprehensive manner. A variety of unknown authors provide the themes for the works, and the texts are key to their understanding. Retablo painters, who give expression to migrants' tales and endow their anecdotes with aesthetic value, also make an important contribution. One of them, Don Vicente Barajas, an old and expert retablo painter from the Bajío, recounts how this became his trade and how he creates each retablo. Ultimately, Jorge Durand and Douglas Massey had the remarkable idea of bringing together the scattered work of these authors and painters, arranging the work to give it coherent conceptual support, and providing an explanation of its sociological significance and aesthetic value.

Retablos have long claimed the attention of many people interested in Mexican plastic arts (notably the great Mexican painters), and because of their efforts some reproductions have been published; however, retablos have never before been used to study social phenomena. At the same time, the issue of workers migrating northward has merited diligent study from many disciplinary viewpoints, employing a variety of methods and approaches; however, never before has there appeared such an extensive unedited rendering of this subject as in the retablos.

This collection of different authors and elements, of diverse motifs and techniques of expression, of aesthetic attraction and sociological analysis, in which academic exposition and popular narrative complement one another without doing an injustice to either, is exceptional; and the combination of all these elements makes this a book that is truly original and of great interest to a wide public.

Dr. Manuel Rodríguez Lapuente
Director, Institute for Social Studies
University of Guadalajara

Acknowledgments
▼▼▼

Any complicated and time-consuming project inevitably owes a debt of thanks to many people, and this book is no exception. We first extend our sincere and heartfelt thanks to the migrants themselves for sharing their innermost thoughts and deepest feelings with us and the rest of the world by depositing a retablo before a revered image. We also express our gratitude to the village artists and humble artisans who gave these sentiments substance by creating small paintings on sheets of tin. Several other people closer to us provided unusual help and support in undertaking the work. Patricia Arias actively participated in the search for retablos and other background materials and provided critical comments during all phases of the study. Héctor Hernández and Víctor Espinoza assisted not only in searching for retablos, but in conducting fieldwork, taking photographs, and carrying out interviews. Susan Ross and David Wicinas read early drafts of the manuscript and made helpful suggestions. We extend our sincere thanks to the many friends, relatives, colleagues, and students who accompanied us on this long adventure, which ultimately, for us, was a labor of love. Finally, we thank the National Institute of Child Health and Human Development, the William and Flora Hewlett Foundation, and the Andrew W. Mellon Foundation, whose financial support made this project possible.

Jorge Durand   Douglas S. Massey
Guadalajara, Jalisco   Chicago, Illinois

Editorial Method
▼▼▼

Throughout this book, but particularly in the concluding chapter, the catalog of the collected retablos, we include the Spanish texts appearing on the retablos and our English translations of those texts. The originals and their accompanying translations presented some unique difficulties; for not only is it almost impossible to translate texts written by semiliterate people in a regional dialect and retain the full flavor and meaning of the original, it is often difficult to accurately transcribe the words themselves. In copying the texts, we generally have attempted to retain the original spelling and punctuation whenever possible.

The principal problem we faced was how to handle upper- and lowercase letters. Some texts clearly distinguished between the two cases, and in these instances we retained the distinction. Other texts were written in odd mixtures of upper- and lowercase, presented entirely in capital letters, or were written with a script that did not distinguish clearly between the two. For ease of reading, in such instances we generally transcribed the text in lowercase letters and put in capitals only where they were grammatically required. However, because accent marks are not customarily used over capital letters in Spanish, in transcribing capitalized letters to lowercase we added accents when necessary. If a text was clearly written in lowercase letters, however, we left accent marks out if they were missing in the original.

In translating the texts, we sought to provide English-speaking readers with clear, accessible, and readable prose. Achieving these goals necessarily involved editing as well as translating. Although we tried to produce literal translations, we often found ourselves choosing words and constructions that, while conveying the underlying meaning accurately, sounded better in English.

We also made grammatical changes and added punctuation, as appropriate. Moreover, in order to clarify the geographical referents for North American readers, we corrected all U.S. place-names from their renderings in phonetic Spanish, and we spelled out the frequent abbreviations of Mexican place-names. Dates were also written out fully in the English translations.

MIRACLES ON THE BORDER

Introduction
▼▼▼

THE MIRACLE OF
MIGRANTS' RETABLOS

t is early morning and the bells in the Church of the Virgin of San Juan de los Lagos are ringing. With the third chime comes the hour to open the main entrance. As the door swings ajar, beggars push forward to occupy their accustomed places on the staircase of the large atrium, and assorted vendors of prints, rosaries, and novena booklets bustle in to set up their booths and stalls. The nuns open up the stand where they will receive the day's alms, and in the sacristy the priest dons his robes to celebrate the day's first mass. On the main altar the sacristan lights candles and checks the chalice to see that it is full; in the sanctuary a never-ending river of people flows into the church. They quietly occupy their places before the altar, as they have since 1769 when the great church was inaugurated to honor the small image of the Virgin brought into town in 1542 by Father Miguel de Bologna.

To one side of the sacristy, in the Virgin's Chamber, the daily presentation of votives begins, fulfilling vows made days, weeks, months, or even years earlier. This is the center to which pilgrims come from throughout the region to leave small paintings on sheets of tin to offer thanks to the Virgin of San Juan de los Lagos for a miracle granted or a favor received. People begin to enter; they cross the room and look intently at the pictures, carefully reading the texts on each one. They discuss the miraculous events quietly among themselves, are amazed, and reflect privately on their import. They look with care for a spot to put their own offerings. From crumpled brown bags they take out their own small paintings wrapped in old newspapers, along with a sketch, and perhaps a photo. With pins and tape they arrange the offerings to form a harmonic whole, so that their miraculous story can be seen and known by all, at least for a time.

As the day progresses, the chamber slowly changes, acquiring a new layer of tokens and mementos. Each day hundreds of thankful supplicants transform the walls of the sanctuary with new votive offerings: drawings, photographs, letters, crutches, bouquets, locks of hair, plaster casts, orthopedic devices, diplomas, drivers' licenses, examination results, and dozens of metal charms in the shape of arms, legs, feet, and hands. In some places, ten or more layers are superimposed on one another, and the offerings are fastened together with tacks, staples, string, and tape. They are stuck to the walls, the floor, and the handrail of the stairway.

Despite the variety of objects and the mixture of colors and textures, one constant stands out in the clutter: the small colorful paintings on sheets of tin. Known as retablos by the common people who leave them, these votive paintings tell the story of a dangerous or threatening event from which the subject has been miraculously delivered through the intervention of a holy image of Christ, the Virgin, or the saints, to whom thanks are reverently offered. This book considers these votive paintings and the meaning they hold for one group of people in particular: Mexican migrants to the United States.

In recent decades the volume of Mexico-United States migration has risen dramatically, and transnational movement has emerged as a major force binding the two countries. During the 1960s, legal immigration to the United States from Mexico rose to 430,000, and in the 1970s this figure grew to more than 680,000 (U.S. Immigration and Naturalization Service 1992). During the 1980s, the flow became truly massive: more than 3 million Mexicans were admitted to the United States as legal immigrants, and another 800,000 arrived without legal documents (Woodrow and Passel 1990). Over the same period, more than 12 million Mexicans entered the United States as temporary visitors (U.S. Immigration and Naturalization Service 1992); and at present more than 13 million people of Mexican origin live north of the border (U.S. Bureau of the Census 1991).

The growing presence of Mexicans in the United States and the extensive movement of people back and forth across the border have attracted considerable attention in both countries. This emerging interest in Mexico-United States migration provides a more than adequate reason to bring retablo painting to the attention of a wider public. Simple, evocative depictions of the dangers and joys of life in the United States and the paradoxes and problems of international movement provide a compelling entrée to this votive art, one that is readily understood by Mexicans and North Americans alike.

Studies of Mexican retablos that have been published in the United States so far have focused primarily on *santos*—small images of Christ, the Virgin, the saints, or other holy images painted on sheets of tin and intended for private devotional use (see Giffords 1974, 1991). Less attention has been paid to *ex-votos*—small votive paintings, also on tin, left at religious shrines to offer public thanks to a divine image for a miracle or favor received. A principal goal of this book is to attract greater attention to votive paintings as meritorious works of popular art.

Of the 81 Mexican retablos published by Gloria Giffords in her seminal book, only 17 were ex-votos (Giffords 1974); and only 10 of the 85 recently assembled by the Meadows Museum of Dallas, Texas, in its exhibition catalog were of this genre (Giffords 1991). Of all the Mexican retablos published in the United States to date, some 84 percent have been santos; and of the 10,000 retablos that Giffords, the leading contemporary scholar of retablo art, personally examined for the Meadows Museum exhibit catalog, only 2.5 percent were ex-votos (Giffords 1991:56). By presenting a large collection of votive retablos that deal with a subject of consuming interest in both Mexico and the United States, we hope to stimulate a greater appreciation for this important genre of popular Mexican art.

A second goal of this volume is to shed light on the origins of votive painting. Although ex-votos and santos share many traits in common, they ultimately arose from different traditions with divergent religious roots. Despite the fact that both genres adopted the same medium—painting on small sheets of tin—ultimately they sought to achieve different ends and employed contrasting styles and varying aesthetic principles. Understanding the distinct historical and religious roots of these two kinds of retablos helps to explain the relatively greater influence of ex-votos on the development of Mexican fine arts, a conundrum that has puzzled Giffords (1974:58).

A third aim of this book is to illuminate the effect of the ex-voto on the theory, practice, and aesthetics of Mexican fine arts during the twentieth century. We describe and analyze the compositional structure, thematic approach, and stylistic conventions of Mexican votive painting. We then trace the influence of these artistic principles on the thinking and work of Mexico's leading artists of the twentieth century, focusing in particular on the work of Frida Kahlo, who owes by far the greatest debt to retablo painting.

In presenting retablos commissioned or painted by Mexican migrants to the United States, we seek not only to achieve artistic goals, but also to understand more deeply an important sociological phenomenon—international migration. By carefully examining ex-votos left at key Mexican religious shrines, we hope to explicate the role that holy images play in the lives of Mexicans living abroad. We believe that these icons—and particularly the Virgin of San Juan de los Lagos—provide a spiritual and cultural anchor for Mexicans in the northern diaspora, giving them a familiar cultural lens through which they can interpret and assimilate the fragmented and often disorienting experiences of life in an alien land.

Finally, we seek to derive new insights into the migratory experience through a careful consideration of the form and content of retablos. We begin by analyzing votive texts to reveal the issues of greatest concern to migrants, and to make explicit the distribution of works by image, date, state of origin in Mexico, and place of destination in the United States. We then present and interpret 40 specific paintings to distill a unique, personalized, and highly colorful view of international migration by those who lived it.

Although Mexico-United States migration has been the subject of countless statistical and ethnographic studies, few have examined it from the viewpoint of the participants themselves (for exceptions, see Gamio 1931; Herrera-Sobek 1979; and Siems 1992). Drawing upon texts and images from migrants' ex-votos, we hope to redress this gap, to construct a fuller picture of the complex process of Mexico-United States migration. In doing so, we depart from the usual mode of social-scientific analysis to follow a lead signalled two decades ago by Gloria Giffords (1974:124): "An examination of all the ex-votos in any one shrine or church would produce a fascinating record of the people's hopes and fears, their thoughts, lives, and experiences, a record more honest than the fullest statistical study."

1
▼▼▼

THE ORIGINS OF VOTIVE PAINTING

There is much confusion among both specialists and the public about the terms *retablo*, *santo*, and *ex-voto*, all of which have been used to denote Mexican religious paintings on tin. Giffords (1974, 1991) refers to santos and ex-votos generically as retablos, but this usage does not accord with that of the people of west-central Mexico, the region where this artistry is now concentrated. Among poor campesinos and humble workers in this region, the words *retablo* and *ex-voto* are used more or less interchangeably to indicate a votive painting on a sheet of tin, with the former generally being preferred in daily conversation. Stylized paintings of the saints, Christ, or the Virgin are called santos or láminas. Because these works have not been produced in Mexico for more than 70 years, however, they are not widely known or appreciated by common people and are rarely discussed except by collectors.

The popular labeling of ex-votos as retablos can be traced back at least to the eighteenth century. Roberto Montenegro's published collection contains one votive dated 1781 that offers thanks to Nuestra Señora de Dolores de Xaltocán for restoring the supplicant's health after a grave illness and ends with the words "en cuia memoria dedica a su Magestad este *Retablo*" (in whose memory he dedicates to her Majesty this *retablo*) (Montenegro 1950:10, emphasis added). The identification of votive paintings as retablos continues throughout the nineteenth century. Giffords

(1974) reproduces an 1825 example that concludes with the words, "por lo cual prometio aser el retablo" (for which I promised to make the retablo); and an 1851 work in the authors' collection ends with the classic phrase "y en reconocimiento de esta maravilla le presento este retablo" (and in recognition of this marvel, I offer the present retablo).

In examining several thousand votive paintings for this book, we almost never found an accompanying text that referred to the work as an ex-voto. Rather, votive paintings on sheets of tin were universally called retablos by the people who painted or commissioned them, a usage that leading figures in Mexican fine arts also adopted (see Atl 1922; Montenegro 1950; Siqueiros 1977; Rivera 1979). In the remainder of this book, therefore, we follow popular Mexican custom and artistic convention by referring to votive paintings on tin simply as retablos, substituting the term *ex-voto* when we wish to distinguish them from santos, which always refer to paintings of saints or other religious figures.

The word *retablo* comes from the Latin *retro-tabula*, or "behind the altar." Originally it referred to decorative or didactic paintings and sculpture placed behind the altar of Catholic churches in the early Middle Ages (Giffords 1974). Later it came to denote reliquary boxes placed at the rear of the altar (de la Maza 1950), and during the twelfth and thirteenth centuries it was generalized to refer to all painted altar panels and frontal pieces (Schroeder 1968; Cousin 1982; Giffords 1991). In a literal sense, therefore, retablos are religious paintings associated with the altar, and under this expansive rubric both ex-votos and santos may be included.

Although ex-votos and santos both arose in association with the Christian altar, their functional roots are quite distinct. Whereas ex-votos arose spontaneously from a deep human desire for divine supplication, santos grew out of the clergy's need for icons to aid in the dissemination of Christianity, the inspiration of piety, and the cultivation of religious fervor, functions especially prominent in the New World. The wealth of the colony of New Spain, as Mexico was called before Independence, and the emotional fervor of mass conversions, especially in the central region, led to a church architecture of ornate apses and gilded transepts that provided an ideal setting for the display of religious paintings and statuary, and during the seventeenth century, the first santos began to be hung on walls surrounding the altars of Mexican churches (Giffords 1991).

Eventually wealthy and pious families began to demand their own paintings of saints for personal use as objects of private devotion. Although artists painted a variety of religious figures and icons, Marian images predominated, and Nuestra Señora del Refugio and the Mater Dolorosa were apparently most popular among affluent patrons of the day (see Giffords 1974:143–44). Other frequently produced images were el Niño de Atocha, el Divino Rostro, San José, la Trinidad, and, of course, Nuestra Señora de Guadalupe.

Spanish colonists and criollos (descendants of Spanish settlers born in the New World) were the earliest patrons of painted santos. Naturally they sought representations of religious images with which they were familiar, generally graphic illustrations from missals, novenas, and other religious books published in Europe. Mexican santos, therefore, were drawn not from the artist's imagination, but were copied from well-known European works of the period. Flemish woodcuts, etchings, and engravings served as the most important models after 1570, when the Spanish Crown granted the Plantin Press of Antwerp a monopoly to supply illustrated religious books to Spain and its colonies (Giffords 1974:32).

Santos are thus stylized copies of European works in which Mexican artists sought to duplicate for home use holy images that were familiar to criollo patrons and acceptable to the Catholic Church for purposes of religious indoctrination. Given the ongoing Counter-Reformation in Mexico and a powerful ecclesiastical hierarchy that displayed little tolerance for religious heterodoxy, the need to portray acceptable images faithfully left little room for originality. Art historians have therefore looked to the details of conception and execution for hints of creativity and imagination (Giffords 1974; Juárez Frías 1991).

Prior to 1800, santos were realized on canvas or wood, but wealthier families began to commission a limited quantity of paintings on copper sheets during the early eighteenth century (Giffords 1974:20). In isolated regions, such as the area of present-day New Mexico, wood continued to be an important medium for santos until modern times (see Steele 1982); and although the use of canvas persisted in Mexico through the mid-nineteenth century, beginning in the 1820s artists in the relatively wealthy and populated west-central states—Jalisco, Guanajuato, and San Luis Potosí—turned to a new medium: tin.

During the late eighteenth century British metallurgists developed a new technique to bond tin leaf to flat iron sheets (Giffords 1974:20). The resulting material was light, durable, relatively rustproof under conditions of low humidity, and paint readily adhered to its smooth surface. Given these attractive properties, Mexican folk artists began relying on tin, which rapidly displaced wood and canvas as the characteristic medium for retablo painting. Because the manufacture of tin plate did not begin in Mexico until 1947, virtually all early santos and ex-votos, as well as most later ones, were painted on sheets imported from Britain or the United States (Giffords 1991:34).

The size of the metal sheets used to produce santos generally followed a standard formula that progressed upward in doubles from 9 square inches (2.5 × 3.5 inches), through 18 and 35 square inches (3.5 × 5 and 5 × 7 inches, respectively), to the most frequently encountered sizes of 70 square inches (7 × 10 inches) and 140 square inches (10 × 14 inches). The very largest santos were painted on sheets of about 280 square inches (14 × 20 inches). This progression in doubles suggests that artists bought large sheets of tin and cut them progressively in half to achieve the desired size (Giffords 1991:37–38).

Santos were generally painted with a limited range of colors (see Giffords 1974:30–31). If a primer coat was used, it tended to be dark—either a solid brown or a red bole. The pictures themselves were rendered using clear reds, dark blues, and yellows. Flesh colors were typically achieved by mixing red oxide or burnt sienna with white. Lettering, when it appeared, was always black, a color also used to represent metal adornments in religious costumes. Although greens appeared occasionally, they were usually dark or olive in tone, and were obtained by using chromium oxide or by mixing yellow and blue. When the cumulative effects of aging, successive layers of varnish, and years of soot are factored in, Mexican santos can often be rather somber.

Santos painted on tin were produced in abundance from the 1820s through the 1920s, with the most prolific period being from 1850 to 1900 (Giffords 1991). Although santos were originally commissioned mainly by affluent criollo patrons, the adoption of tin plate as an artistic medium during the nineteenth century reduced the cost substantially and made them accessible to middle-class mestizos (people of mixed European and Amerindian origins). As they began to be adopted by a broader cross section of Mexican society, painted santos declined in popularity among the elite.

During the 100 years of their production, the style of santos remained relatively static, and there was little artistic innovation or experimentation within the genre. According to Giffords, "The retablo santo artist was a copyist" (1991:40), and "basically . . . [santos] are copies of other works" (1974:34). The religious figures depicted in santo paintings "strictly follow the church's official, predetermined iconography, or conventional imagery" (Giffords 1974:28).

The genre's demise came during the early twentieth century when industrial processes enabled the mass production of cheap prints of religious images from lithographs and steel engravings. These reproductions catered to popular tastes for greater realism and brighter colors. As demand fell among the elite and the masses switched to cheaper and more colorful products, the quality and workmanship of painted santos declined until production finally ceased sometime in the 1920s (Giffords 1974:44).

Mexican santo painting, thus arising from evangelical roots, supplied icons to devout members of an elite criollo class (and only later to mestizos) during a brief 100-year period. They were painted on small sheets of tin in a subdued style using a limited range of dark colors, and they adhered closely to European iconographic conventions approved by the Catholic Church. Because santos followed a rigid formula tied to a static society, they disappeared when industrialization and revolution transformed the countryside, and thus society, to create modern Mexico. As an art form, santos have been extinct for three generations.

The ex-voto grew from very different roots and arose to satisfy deeper human needs using a flexible artistic style that was not wedded to a particular time or place. As Mexican society changed, the content and execution of ex-votos evolved, and these paintings have remained a vital part of the Mexican popular artistic scene. Whereas santos arose from a conservative institution's need to evangelize and an elite's desire to objectify its piety, ex-votos arose from a spontaneous desire on the part of the people to placate supernatural forces they believed controlled their fates.

The Latin term *ex-voto* means "from a vow," suggesting the use of these paintings as tokens of payment for divine favors sought or received (Egan 1991). Because votive painting has its roots in pre-Christian practices, Mexican priests have always been ambivalent, and at times hostile, toward this popular artistic tradition (Reavis 1992:191–204; Giffords 1991:58).

The human need to communicate with the divine transcends temporal and cultural boundaries, however, and the practice of the leaving of objects to supplicate or thank a deity has very ancient roots (Egan 1991). Throughout history, votive offerings have provided a key point of articulation between humans and their gods. Although the placing of votive objects at religious shrines is now closely associated with Christianity and the Catholic Church, it has older roots in the pagan traditions of both Europe and Mesoamerica.

Archaeological evidence reveals that the ancient Greeks, Romans, Etruscans, Iberians, and

Gauls all possessed well-developed votive traditions (Decouflé 1964; Egan 1991). In these ancient cultures it was common practice to acknowledge or pray for the restoration of health by leaving small figures of clay, wax, wood, or stone shaped like hands, eyes, arms, legs, feet, or vital organs at shrines. Although historians of medicine have long found these votive objects interesting as sources of information about the degree of anatomical knowledge among the ancients (see Decouflé 1964), it was not until the mid-nineteenth century that collectors began to appreciate their worth as pieces of popular art and museums took an interest in their conservation and restoration (Creux 1979).

In the ancient Aegean, these offerings were often accompanied by plaques that contained the name of the god being invoked along with a prayer of thanks for achieving some notable passage in life (Sánchez Lara 1990). Written offerings, however, were exceptional among the ancients, and the first Christian votives, like their pagan counterparts, consisted primarily of small anatomical figures made of wax, wood, marble, or metal (Sánchez Lara 1990). The tokens were deposited at sites that had long served as foci of veneration in the pagan world, but which had been converted to Christian uses during the fourth and fifth centuries A.D. (Romandía de Cantú 1978; Egan 1991).

During the fifteenth century, the long-standing practice of leaving anatomical tokens as votive objects gave way to a more elaborate display of gratitude and adoration: the painted ex-voto. Votive paintings first appeared in Italy at the end of the 1400s. Growing out of the Italian Renaissance, this new votive practice spread rapidly throughout the Mediterranean and ultimately diffused to the rest of continental Europe (Cousin 1982; Egan 1991). The immediate antecedents of painted ex-votos were religious altar paintings on canvas or wood that depicted scenes from the life of Christ, the saints, or other biblical figures (Cousin 1982; Sánchez Lara 1990). Often the wealthy patron who commissioned the works was incorporated as a participant in the scene.

The painted ex-voto permitted the introduction of new visual elements to the votive tradition—human action, divine images, and a textual explanation of events—elements that had been implicit in the anatomical votives of the ancients (Cousin 1982). The new votive pictures typically included a rendering of the miraculous event, a representation of the holy image responsible for the miracle, and a text that not only identified the beneficiary by name, but specified the date and place of the happening. With the emergence of painted ex-votos, therefore, retablos passed from being mere archaeological artifacts to being authentic historical documents.

Although the tradition of the painted ex-voto began among the wealthy, its popularity gradually increased and spread to humbler sectors of European society (Palais Lascaris 1987). Whereas votive pictures commissioned by wealthy patrons were typically executed on a large scale and entrusted to well-established artists (including such luminaries as Gonzaga and Rafael—see Sánchez Lara 1990), less affluent patrons usually requested ex-votos of smaller size and lower quality. Often these objects were realized by painters of second or third rank, and frequently by humble artisans who were simply handy with a brush.

As retablo painting developed and spread throughout Europe, it eventually reached the New World. Votive works were probably first brought into Mexico by Spanish soldiers. Indeed, the great conquistador himself, Hernán Cortez, upon being bitten by a scorpion in Yautepec, Morelos, commended himself to the Virgin of Guadalupe (of Extremadura, not Tepeyac) and promised to prepare a votive offering if he survived his misfortune (Egan 1991). Cortez kept his promise and ordered the goldsmiths of Azcapotzalco to fashion an ex-voto containing forty emeralds and two pearls set in a gold box that housed the remnants of the poisonous insect that dared to attack the conqueror of Mexico (Valle Arizpe 1941).

The spread of painted retablos in the New World was slow at first. In order to prevent the formation of independent bases of power in New Spain, the Crown regularly rotated colonial officials back and forth between Mexico City and Madrid (Benítez 1965). For a time, therefore, Spanish soldiers and bureaucrats followed long-established habits and placed ex-votos in peninsular sanctuaries upon their return. One such offering (though from a later period) expresses the thanks of a Catalonian sailor who survived the Battle of Callao in Peru on May 2, 1866, the last attempt by the Spanish Crown to reestablish hegemony in the New World (seen by Jorge Durand in Barcelona, 1990).

Another reason for the slow emergence of votive painting was the simple lack of Mexican religious sanctuaries where offerings could be left. A full century passed between the fall of the Aztec capital of Tenochtitlán in 1521 and the construction of the first shrine to the Virgin of Guadalupe at Tepeyac in 1622 (Lafaye 1976:243). It was only after the criollo society became truly rooted in the New World and built its own churches and shrines, finding that periodic returns to Spain were no longer common or feasible, that votive traditions became firmly established in Mexico.

In transplanting the art of retablo painting to Mexican soil, of course, the Spanish conquerors did not encounter a cultural vacuum; votive practices were well known in Mesoamerica before the conquest. According to one sixteenth-century chronicler, Clavijero, "The most important duty of the priest, and the Mexicans' principal religious ceremony, consisted in making offerings and sacrifices on certain occasions to obtain a favor from heaven or thanks for favors received" (cited in Montenegro 1950).

Objective evidence of pre-Hispanic votive traditions is found in the Mexican archaeological record. The earliest known votive figure, now in New York's Brooklyn Museum, is an Olmec carving that dates from the period 800–500 B.C.; it consists of a male image sculpted in jade and holding a masked child in his arms (Townsend 1992). Mexico's National Museum of Anthropology has two likely votive pieces in its collection: one of small size in the form of a leg, and the other of large size and more elaborately constructed in the form of a spinal column; both are of Zapotec origin from Monte Albán and date from the period 100 B.C. to 400 A.D. (Solís 1991). The Amparo Museum of Puebla and the Archaeological Museum of Taxco also contain pre-Hispanic ceramic objects shaped in the form of feet (viewed by Jorge Durand in 1991); the piece in Taxco is again of Zapotec origin. Sánchez Lara (1990) believes that many of the carved females from the classic period, often referred to as pretty women, are actually votive objects linked to fertility.

Despite the existence of pre-Hispanic votive traditions, the practice of votive painting never really took hold among Mexico's indigenous populations after the Conquest. Although expressions of pre-Hispanic religiosity were tolerated by Catholic missionaries, they were not encouraged, and priests instead sought to insert European practices into the native spiritual milieu (Lafaye 1976). In regions of Mexico dominated by Amerindians, such as Oaxaca, Chiapas, and Michoacán, evangelization encouraged native traditions of dance, music, and crafts but discouraged votive traditions that competed directly with European Christian rituals.

Votive painting ultimately became most firmly established among Mexico's mestizos, in whom pre-Hispanic sentiments were united with European styles and techniques in a way that did not threaten the sensibilities of the Catholic Church. The practice of votive painting first emerged, however, among criollos in and around the Valley of Mexico during the early colonial era (Giffords 1974:119).

Mexico City was the seat of criollo power and the point of introduction of most European cultural innovations. As in Europe, painted votives here grew out of altar paintings of biblical scenes commissioned for didactic purposes. As Roberto Montenegro explains, "When transforming the old religion the missionaries followed a tradition adopted from time immemorial by the nobles of Europe: they commissioned from artists pictures of miracles and included themselves in the pictures standing beside the saint and giving him thanks. Such was the origin of these votive pictures" (1950:11).

Dating the precise beginnings of votive painting in Mexico is difficult because the earliest works were painted on perishable media such as canvas or wood and have not survived. In Europe, Cousin (1982) circumvented this problem by using better-known works by established artists; these larger works themselves included depictions of retablos. From the dates assigned to these paintings, he roughly estimated the beginnings of votive painting in the Old World. Thus, a 1570 painting by Titian shows a cathedral altar with votive paintings attached, suggesting that painted ex-votos were present in Europe by the latter half of the sixteenth century (Cousin 1982).

A comparable indicator for Mexico comes from a series of engravings of the Virgin of Guadalupe done by the Belgian artist Samuel Stradanus between 1604 and 1622 (Orendain 1948; Genaro Cuadriello 1989; Sánchez Lara 1990). In the most celebrated print, executed around 1615, the Virgin is shown on an altar positioned at the center of the composition, and attached near her nimbus are several anatomical ex-votos in the shape of legs, heads, and hands. To either side hang four painted ex-votos, each with an explanatory text that recounts a miraculous happening.

One of the miracles recounted on these early votives tells the story of the sacristan Juan Pavón who, according to the text, "had a child with a bad abscess in the throat and he anointed him with oil from the lamp of Our Lady and he was cured without further action" (Genaro Cuadriello 1989). Thus, despite the fact that some scholars, such as Ramírez (1990), place the emergence of painted votives in the eighteenth century, indirect evidence suggests earlier origins at the beginning of the seventeenth century.

The oldest works of votive content that have survived to the present are several large oil paintings that can today be found in ecclesiastical museums. The Museum of the Basilica of Guadalupe, for example, contains an ex-voto commissioned by Don Antonio Carbajal from the end of the seventeenth century; it thanks the Virgin of Guadalupe for saving his son, who fell from a horse and was dragged along the ground with his foot still in the stirrup (Genaro Cuadriello 1989:93). Another painting from the same museum might be considered to be a votive of supplication; it shows a procession of children beseeching the Virgin to lift a plague that struck Mexico City in 1544 (Genaro Cuadriello 1989:90–91). One final votive comes from the Cathedral of San Luis Potosí. Dated 1693, it offers thanks from Don Diego de Acevedo, the city's mayor, for the miracle of recovering from a serious illness that had left him near death (Casa de Cultura 1991).

Unfortunately, smaller and more popular ex-votos from the period have not been preserved. The earliest popular retablo that we managed to locate comes from the mid-eighteenth century. Painted on wood and dated 1743, it tells the story of Don Ignacio Antonio de Castro Tobio, the mayor of Texcoco (in the Valley of Mexico), and his companion Don Pedro de Castaños Giel Barrio, whose carriage overturned on the road from the village of Tepetlastoc. According to the text, "The mules dragged them along a great distance, and, invoking for the third time the miraculous image of Our Lady of Tulantongo, the traces of the mule on the whip side were broken, both of them came to a halt, and their lives were saved, without serious injury, all due to the Mother of God" (Montenegro 1950:1).

These and other early votive paintings come mainly from sanctuaries located in and around Mexico City (see the place-names mentioned in the seventeenth- and eighteenth-century retablos reproduced in Montenegro [1950] and Giffords [1974]). Over time, however, the practice of votive painting spread to the north and west, following the path of criollo settlement and cultural dominance, into the states of Querétaro, Guanajuato, Jalisco, Zacatecas, and San Luis Potosí.

By the latter half of the eighteenth century, examples of votive painting began to be common throughout western Mexico. In his study of the well-known regional painter Hermenegildo Bustos, for example, Aceves Barajas (1956) reproduces a retablo from Guanajuato dated 1766; and Montenegro (1950:14), in his classic study, presents a retablo dated 1798 and dedicated to Nuestra Señora de la Salud, of Pátzcuaro, Michoacán. The Museum of the Alhóndiga in Guanajuato has in its collection a retablo dated 1822 and dedicated to el Señor de Villaseca, whose church is located just outside the city.

Thus, by the end of the eighteenth century the practice of painting ex-votos had spread from the Valley of Mexico to become prominent in the west-central region of the country. Several characteristics of these early votive works suggest their criollo origins. First, the clothing worn by the figures is invariably European in style and upper-class in appearance. Second, the text is always written in Spanish with frequent errors of spelling and punctuation, because literacy of any sort was not common outside the criollo class in eighteenth-century Mexico. Third, the rooms depicted in the paintings and the accoutrements reveal a level of affluence far above the poverty typical of mestizos and Indians at the time. Fourth, in cases where the votaries are identified by title, the position given suggests elite membership (e.g., the mayors of Texcoco and San Luis Potosí). Finally, to the extent that color can be accurately discerned in old paintings, the figures appear to be light skinned.

Over the course of the nineteenth century, however, the Mexican tradition of votive painting underwent two important changes. First, there was shift in the class background and ethnic origins of both patrons and clients. The introduction of tinplate in the nineteenth century provided a cheap and versatile medium that displaced canvas and wood and opened retablos to broader social participation (Giffords 1974, 1991). Although the demand for paintings on tin spread first to the middle class, by the late 1800s it was also in common use among the lower classes, who were predominantly mestizo. As with the painted santo, once ex-votos were taken up by the masses, they became unfashionable among the elite; and over the course of the twentieth century the clothing, settings, subjects, and physical types depicted in Mexican retablos have become increasingly popular and mestizo in nature.

Second, the geographic center of retablo painting shifted away from the Valley of Mexico toward the west-central region of the country. By the 1920s, the production of votive art had become concentrated in a few key western states, notably Guanajuato, Jalisco, San Luis Potosí, and Zacatecas. Outside of these areas votive sentiments remained strong, but they were no longer expressed so frequently in pictorial form. Instead, pilgrims satisfied their needs for supplication using *milagros*, small charms fashioned in the shape of feet, hands, legs, arms, heads, or other anatomical shapes.

In the colonial period, milagros were manufactured by skilled silversmiths for elite clients. Ultimately, however, they came to be mass produced for humbler families using tin and other base metals. In fact, milagros continue to be popular in Mexico today and are found in profusion throughout the republic (Giffords 1991; Egan 1991). In addition to anatomical shapes, recent additions to the inventory of milagros include houses, pistols, bottles, animals, planes, automobiles, and just about anything else used by human beings.

Another form of votive expression of European origin still observed in Mexico is the book of miraculous texts. In the Chapel of San Sebastián de Aparicio in Puebla, there is an example of an altar book in which pilgrims make public vows and write texts giving thanks for miracles granted. In the Chapel of la Noria, on the highway between Mexico City and Querétaro, a similar book exists, and devout truckers stop to leave messages and fasten images of their patron saints. The drivers have also decorated the altar with a more unusual votive display: hundreds of fluorescent, triangular road markers that glow brightly whenever light strikes them.

Despite the widespread geographic distribution and persistent popularity of milagros and other votive objects, retablo painting is now confined largely to Mexico's west-central states; and within this region, it expresses the values and sentiments of the masses rather than the elite. Thus, a genre of didactic religious painting originally imported by European priests for evangelical purposes was transformed into an indigenous votive practice by criollo colonists acting on an impulse ultimately derived from the pagan cultures of Europe. It was then appropriated by middle- and lower-class mestizos in whom the pagan drives of Europe connected with a powerful votive impulse inherited from the pre-Hispanic world (Charlot 1949:139).

In essence, Mexican retablo painting represents the application of old-world techniques to a new-world medium in order to satisfy a deep human need for supplication rooted in the ancient cultures of Europe and America. Although votive painting had diffused widely throughout the Catholic world by the end of the seventeenth century, the art achieved its fullest development and greatest expression in Mexico, and only there has it continued as a thriving artistic tradition.

In Europe, painted ex-votos declined in popularity during the nineteenth century and all but disappeared by 1900 (Cousin 1982; Palais Lascaris 1987). Even at the peak of their popularity, the number of ex-votos produced in Europe paled in comparison with the quantity manufactured in Mexico. A census carried out by Cousin (1982) in the French region of Provence, for example, enumerated a total of only 4,016 ex-votos produced in the three centuries from 1660 to 1960. These votive works were distributed among 128 churches and five museums. Two churches that housed a relatively large number of votive paintings—Notre Dame de Lumières and Notre Dame de Consolation a Hyères—contained only 341 and 378 ex-votos, respectively.

In contrast, a systematic count of ex-votos conducted in just one relatively small Mexican sanctuary in 1924 (el Señor de la Misericordia in Tepatitlán de Morelos, Jalisco) identified some 1,052 retablos produced over the prior 100 years (cited in Orendain 1948). The total number of votive paintings deposited at major Mexican pilgrimage sites—such as the Church of San Juan de los Lagos—must be in the hundreds of thousands. One retablo painter whom we interviewed stated that he alone had painted more than 5,000 ex-votos in his lifetime, mostly dedicated to the Virgin of San Juan (Durand and Massey 1990).

On any given day scores of recently deposited retablos are on display at popular Mexican pilgrimage sites, and the number of new arrivals is so great that it creates problems of disposal for priests who must somehow cope with the excess. What becomes of surplus retablos is uncertain. According to Giffords (1991:58), priests at the church of San Juan de los Lagos regularly sell off old works to antique dealers. In our own fieldwork, however, we have uncovered at least one instance in which votive paintings from the Church of San Juan were deposited in a field and left to rust. When an enterprising antique dealer attempted to remove them, he was stopped by a priest and forced to unload those he had gathered back onto the pile, where they continued to deteriorate.

If many surplus retablos are preserved, it is also clear that many are lost. In some cases, priests seeking to "modernize" chapels have partially or totally destroyed a stock of retablos that had accumulated over many years (this recently occurred at the shrine of el Cristo del Cubilete, in Guanajuato). More common, however, is the ruin that arises from benign neglect, which is apparently the case at the sanctuary of the Virgin of Zapopan. Moreover, as retablos have become increasingly valuable to collectors, robbery has become distressingly common, and we have personally seen paintings disappear overnight from sanctuary walls (including some photographed for this volume). In some cases—as at the shrines to el Niño de Atocha, el Señor de la Misericordia, and el Señor de Villaseca—parochial authorities have had to mount new security efforts to preserve their artistic patrimony.

European and Mexican votive paintings differ not only in quantity, but also in content. In Europe, maritime themes—shipwrecks, storms, being lost at sea—are exceedingly common as subjects of votive art (Cousin 1982); but because Mexican votive painting took root in the land-locked central plateau region, these themes are largely absent from its retablos. Roberto Montenegro (1950:17) reproduces one seafaring retablo from 1840, in which Doña María Gertrudes Castañeda gives thanks for surviving a tempest that befell her shortly after setting sail from Mexico, but it is the only such example published to date. In fact, among the thousands of retablos we examined for this study, we encountered only one with a vaguely maritime character, that of a poor fisherman who thanked the Virgin of San Juan for his being saved from a sudden storm on Lake Chapala, Jalisco.

Despite the general absence of maritime themes in Mexican votive painting, they are not missing from Mexico's votive tradition altogether. Deliverance from potential catastrophe at sea continues to be commemorated with milagros deposited in shrines along Mexico's Caribbean coast. Oettinger (1991:viii), for example, found that "in coastal churches of southeastern México, grateful sailors offer wooden ships, many replete with tiny, hand-carved crew members, in gratitude for a saint's protection during a storm at sea."

Another European motif not well represented among Mexican retablos is that of the penitent. In France it was common for penitents or groups of pilgrims to commemorate a journey to a sacred site by leaving an individual or collective ex-voto (Palais Lascaris 1987). Typically the painted scene showed a supplicant, a religious fraternity, or group of friends making their way to a shrine and praying before a sacred image. Even though religious pilgrimages are very common in Mexico, they are generally not associated with votive art.

San Juan de los Lagos is an important destination for pilgrims, and arriving penitents often leave printed images, flags, and standards of various sorts to identify their religious affiliation; but they do not leave painted ex-votos. The closest example we personally encountered was a retablo prepared by a union member to thank the Virgin of San Juan on behalf of his fellow workers for the steady progress they had made in their vocation. The only penitent work that turned up in our investigations was the painting *Procession of the Children Against the Plague of Cocolixtli*, dated 1544 and preserved in the Museum of the Basilica of Guadalupe (Genaro Cuadriello 1989:90–91).

Although seafaring and penitent themes are generally absent from Mexican votive art, other subjects are similar to those found in Europe. An eight-category typology of votive themes developed by Creux (1979) to study Swiss and German ex-votos can be applied reasonably well to Mexican votive works: sickness, catastrophe, war, fire, falling, work, animals, and thanksgiving. The latter category is the simplest and most basic, consisting only of a person kneeling in front of a divine image; in both Europe and Mexico it is the most common.

Technical and stylistic features also link European and Mexican ex-votos. On both continents artists divide the pictorial space into separate sections corresponding to different points in time—before, during, and after the miraculous happening. Another common device is to display all members of a supplicant's family within the painting; sometimes five, ten, fifteen, or twenty people are shown lined up and giving thanks to the holy image. Finally, in both European and Mexican ex-votos, figures are frequently shown appealing to multiple images, which are arrayed across the top of the painting (compare the paintings reproduced in Creux [1979] and Garduño Pulido et al. [1990]).

Votive traditions are also known throughout the rest of Latin America, but painted ex-votos have not attained the same level of popularity or artistic development as in Mexico. In this region, votive sentiments are expressed largely in the form of objects left before sacred images at popular pilgrimage sites. These votive articles may include orthopedic devices, documents, photographs, items of clothing, tresses, toys, and other items, but by far the most common votive object is the milagro, the small metallic charm rendered in anatomical shapes (Egan 1991).

In Peru, the principal images of supplication are la Virgen de la Leche in Cuzco and la Virgen del Rosario in Lima, both of which are associated with a long and rich tradition of supplication using milagros made of silver and realized with great artistry by master craftsmen (see Egan 1991). Folk artists in Ayacucho continue to produce objects called retablos that are made of wood and consist of free-standing scenes of brightly colored figures enclosed in a shallow rectangular box with doors that open outward from the front (Sordo 1990). Although these retablos began as religious offerings associated with the altar, eventually they evolved into a new form that focuses on scenes from daily life and responds increasingly to a demand from tourists and collectors. At present, Peruvian retablos seem to have lost their votive character entirely.

Residents of other Andean countries also use milagros to express votive sentiments. In Ecuador, the image of Nuestra Señora de Santa Agua in the town of Baños is adorned with thousands of such charms; and la Virgen de las Lajas and la Virgen de Chiquinquira attract pilgrims from all over Colombia. In Bolivia, metallic milagros cover images of the Virgin found in Oruro, Socavón, Sucre, and Copacabana, with the latter being the most important pilgrimage site in that region. Further south, votive practices are associated with la Virgen del Carmen in Chile; la Virgen de Luján in Argentina; la Virgen de los Treinta y Tres in Uruguay; and Nuestra Señora de Caacupe in Paraguay (Polanco Brito 1984; Egan 1991).

Votive practices are also known in several countries of Central America. In Guatemala, the faithful use milagros to pay their respects to el Cristo Negro at the sanctuary of Nuestro Señor de Esquipulas. In Cartago, Costa Rica, the Basilica of Nuestra Señora de los Angeles houses a small Indian image of la Virgen Negrita (the little black Virgin) that is perpetually covered with milagros and other offerings. In Honduras, the leading votive shrine is dedicated to Nuestra Señora de Suyupa; in Nicaragua to la Inmaculada Concepción; and in El Salvador, to Nuestra Señora de la Paz; all attract milagros by the thousands (Polanco Brito 1984; Egan 1991:15–16).

Votive traditions also persist in the Caribbean. Although painted ex-votos are no longer produced in the Dominican Republic (where milagros are still common), the Sanctuary of Higuey does contain 16 votive paintings dating from the late sixteenth century. They are painted on wood medallions and the oldest, created exactly one hundred years after Columbus's arrival, tells the story of Isidro Alvarez, who on his way to Yaguana, "got lost five leagues out to sea, and commending himself to Our Lady everyone escaped and they gave thanks to God in the year 1592" (Polanco Brito 1984).

Elsewhere in the Caribbean, milagros are left in payment for promises made to specific images for particular favors expected or received. According to Vidal (1972), in Puerto Rico supplicants turn to an image of San Blas for problems with the throat or neck; to San Bartolomé or San Ramón for problems of fertility or childbirth; and to la Virgen de Montserrat or la Virgen del Carmen for the full range of trials and tribulations. In return for answered prayers, Puerto Ricans express their gratitude not only by depositing the milagros before a holy image, but also by wearing them around their necks (see Egan 1991; Vidal 1972).

In Cuba the chief recipient of votive supplication is la Virgen de la Caridad del Cobre in Havana, which over the years has attracted votaries from many quarters (Polanco Brito 1984). Upon winning the Nobel Prize for literature in 1954, for example, Ernest Hemingway, then a resident of Cuba, deposited his medal at this shrine as an offering of thanks to the image for its favor (Baker 1969).

Votive practices are also common in Brazil. A shrine to Nosso Senhor do Bomfim, in the coastal community of São Salvador de Bahía, is well described by the novelist Jorge Amado, a native of the city: "Pictures by the score, legs, hands, arms, and wax heads, depictions of terrible accidents, fill this insane hall which is the strangest museum one can possibly imagine.

Rich offerings and poor offerings, large *milagros* and small *milagros*. The Senhor do Bomfim is a recorder of miracles" (Amado 1966 [cited in Egan 1991]).

In the United States votive practices occur primarily in areas of Latino settlement close to the Mexico-United States border. Gamio (1930:122) describes a small private shrine in San Antonio, Texas, run by an old woman, that attracted a multitude of faithful pilgrims during the 1920s. The Cathedral of San Fernando, also in San Antonio and the oldest cathedral in the United States, contains an image of el Señor de Esquipulas (of Guatemala) that continues to draw supplicants from all over Texas who express their thanks to the image through milagros, photographs, and other offerings. The sanctuary of la Virgen de San Juan del Valle, just north of the Mexico-Texas border in the Rio Grande valley, also attracts votaries who leave objects such as romantic mementos, tresses of hair, crutches, wax figures, wood carvings, and thousands of letters and photographs.

A distinctive tradition in the border region is the supplication of "victim-intercessors," historical figures who are neither divine nor sainted but who are believed to possess powers of intervention (Griffith 1987). Victim-intercessors are *almas*, or souls, of common people whose lives were taken through deception, usually by someone of higher social standing (Griffith 1992:105–115). Although victims of an unjust society, they are believed to have been judged innocent by God and to be able to return as apparitions to help common people in trouble. Although victim-intercessors behave like saints in the minds of the people, they are not recognized as such by the Catholic Church.

Perhaps the best-known figure is Juan Soldado, whose real name was Juan Castillo Morales (Griffith 1992:112–114). Juan Soldado translates roughly as "G.I. Joe," and according to legend he was a private in the Mexican Army stationed in Tijuana. His commanding officer (the rank varies from Captain to General depending on the narrator) committed a terrible crime (in some versions raping and murdering a little girl who came to camp with food or laundry) and then accused Private Juan of the despicable act. The officer had Juan arrested and, in order to keep him from testifying in his own defense, shot him "while he was trying to escape" (a lamentably common practice through the early twentieth century known as *la ley de fuga*, or "the law of flight").

Shortly after his death, however, Juan Soldado began appearing, first to his mother, then to other women keeping watch at his grave, and finally to the officer himself, who confessed his treachery and died. Over the years, Juan Soldado became known as a source of succor for poor people in need of assistance in a hostile world, and numerous miracles have been attributed to him. His devotees have erected a crude chapel made of scrap lumber at his grave site in Tijuana (which the Catholic Church does not support, because it does not recognize him as a saint). Other private chapels honoring Juan Soldado are found along highways and in storefronts along the border region stretching from the Pacific to the Rio Grande (Griffith 1992:112–115).

Other victim-intercessors popular in the area include Pedro Blanco, a soldier who was murdered one night in the 1920s in Nogales, Sonora, as he walked home with some unusually large gambling winnings in his pocket; and Jesús Malverde, a bandit who lived in Sinaloa and was hanged in Culiacán on May 5, 1909 (Griffith 1992:105–115). Malverde continues to be revered as the "patron saint to contemporary thieves and smugglers" (Escobedo 1989:147), and his popularity has grown recently with the emergence of Culiacán as a major staging area for the shipment of drugs into the United States. All three figures—Juan Soldado, Jesús Malverde, and Pedro Blanco—developed traditions of votive supplication, and the first two almas continue to attract a strong following; Pedro Blanco's reputation as a miracle worker appears to be dying out (Griffith 1992:111).

As can be seen from the preceding discussion, votive sentiments remain a constant throughout Latin America; but the absence of painted ex-votos in most regions underscores the uniqueness of Mexico's artistic achievement. Although Spain transmitted similar cultural practices and religious rituals to all of its colonies, votive painting achieved its greatest popularity, longest continuous practice, and highest level of artistic development in Mexico, and only there does votive painting constitute a flourishing artistic tradition.

2

▼▼▼

RETABLOS IN THEORY
AND PRACTICE

The common feature of all santos and ex-votos—and the source of much confusion between them—is that both genres are painted on pieces of tin that have been reduced down from larger sheets by a progressive cutting in half (Giffords 1991:37–38). As with santos, ex-votos are rectangular in shape, with the largest at about 280 square inches (14 × 20 inches) and the smallest around 18 square inches (3.5 × 5 inches). The most common sizes are 140 square inches (10 × 14 inches) and 70 square inches (7 × 10 inches) (Giffords 1974, 1991; Orendain 1948). Aside from being painted on tin, however, Mexican santos and ex-votos share little in common. In their conceptualization, philosophy, and execution, the two genres are opposite in nearly every way. Whereas santos faithfully reproduce European icons approved by the Church, ex-votos depict a range of situations from daily life. Whereas santos allow little room for individual creativity and innovation, ex-votos encourage novelty and personal expression. Whereas santos adhere to rigid stylistic and iconographic conventions, ex-votos follow a flexible artistic format and broad compositional guidelines.

Mexican votive paintings are composed of three basic elements: a holy image, a graphic rendering of a threatening occurrence or miraculous event, and a text explaining what happened (Giffords 1974, 1991). The holy image is usually depicted suspended in clouds and located to one side of the composition. Although the representation of the holy image must bear some relation to official iconography, the rules of interpretation are loose rather than rigid. In order to function effectively within the context of an ex-voto, a holy image need only convey identity in general terms. A variety of colors, styles, shapes, props, and levels of detail may be used to depict a holy image, as long as an overall gestalt of recognition is achieved.

Strict reproduction of a holy image is less important in ex-votos than in santos because the action itself is the focus of the work and its raison d'être. Moreover, because votive paintings are left at specific shrines, the identity of the image is usually obvious from the context in which it is placed (votives to the Virgin of Talpa are usually not deposited before the Virgin of San Juan de los Lagos, for example). Finally, any doubt about the identity of an image is usually dispelled by the text, which typically refers to the image by name.

In Mexican retablos, textual material is generally found at the bottom of the work. In addition to thanking the holy image, the text normally states the place of origin of the donor along with the date, place, and circumstances of the event, and gives an account of the miraculous intervention of the divine being. Expressions of gratitude draw upon a standard vocabulary of faith and devotion that has evolved over scores of years and thousands of pilgrimages. Most texts begin with the words *doy gracias* (I give thanks) and express a heartfelt need to *hacer patente* (make known) the miraculous results of a divine intervention. In the text, the supplicant states that at the moment of crisis, *me encomendé a la Virgen* (I entrusted myself to the Virgin) and tell how *me concedió el milagro* (she granted me the miracle). They often end with the simple statement that *por eso dedico el presente retablo* (for that reason I dedicate the present retablo).

The length and detail of votive texts set Mexican retablos distinctly apart from their European counterparts. In Europe, votive narration is plain and unadorned; in many cases, the text is pared to its bare essentials, containing just the word *ex-voto*, together with the date (often only the year) and the donor's name or initials (Jakovsky 1949; Cousin 1982; Orendain 1948; Palais Lascaris 1987). At times the text is eliminated entirely, and in this case European ex-votos devolve to a two-part compositional structure rather than the three-part organization typical of Mexico.

In Mexican retablos, the largest, most important, and central portion of the pictorial space is the depiction of the miraculous event. In rendering the dangerous or threatening circumstances under which the divine intervention occurred, there are no rigid rules and few strict protocols.

According to one art historian, "The imagination of the artist has ample scope to express the supernatural and divine intervention that is superimposed on logical reality and only is acceptable in terms of a blind and irrational faith" (Moyssén 1965:26). The principal desideratum is that the artistic devices used in the execution of the ex-voto heighten the emotional intensity of the moment and emphasize the ongoing drama of events.

Although the choice of materials, styles, and methods is open and flexible, several techniques have become conventional over the years. In identifying these techniques, we do not argue that retablo artists have joined together to form a "school of retablo art," or that they self-consciously select "retablo painting techniques." Indeed, many of the devices they employ represent common solutions to fundamental artistic problems that are widely employed by untrained artists throughout the world. We simply assert that among retablo painters in Mexico, artistic sensibilities and methods have evolved to yield a set of identifiable traits that have now become characteristic of the genre.

First, Mexican ex-voto artists rely heavily on bold, bright colors to augment the emotional effect of the scene. Unlike santos, which are often rather dark and somber, ex-votos are typically luminous and vibrant. In order to convey the power of extreme circumstances, Mexican retablo painters make full use of the color spectrum. Luxurious reds, deep blues, luminous golds, pale pastels, translucent greens, pure whites, and bright yellows abound in votive paintings. Although scenes of family members gathered around a sick bed may occasionally be rendered in subdued tones, the colors are rarely dark. Actions and dramatic events are almost always presented in vivid colors. Background detail is frequently painted using divergent hues to add emotional power to the composition, and the figures themselves are often rendered in contrasting tones.

Second, Mexican votive painters undertake a deliberate and self-conscious manipulation of space in order to underscore the drama of the unfolding events. Scale and proportion are sacrificed to intensify emotion; angles become sharper and perspective awkward in order to increase the dramatic power of a scene. The helplessness of mortals in the face of a dire situation is captured by juxtaposing tiny human figures with larger-than-life holy images (in real life, many sacred figures are rather small). The bewildering nature of the moment is enhanced by a surreal placement of figures, props, and background constructions.

Third, Mexican votive painters systematically segment, deconstruct, and reorder time.

Events that occurred sequentially are broken down into representative instants and shown simultaneously. Different stages in the progress of a miraculous happening are arranged within a common pictorial frame. Supplicants shown in the throes of a dire circumstance in one part of a retablo are pictured offering thanks to the image in another. Actions occurring before, during, and after the miracle are shuffled and recombined for maximum psychological effect.

Fourth, theater props and stage motifs are used from time to time to emphasize the drama of unfolding events. Action takes place on crude stages erected magically in the picture space; curtains are pulled back to reveal figures in critical situations; lush and lustrous fabrics are draped over walls and furniture as if in a set; actors appear to perform before audiences of horrified onlookers; cinematic techniques such as the flashback and fast forward are employed to move about in time.

Finally, over the course of the twentieth century, Mexican ex-votos have increasingly incorporated a variety of materials and techniques in their construction to create collages that blend traditional painting with modern media. Photographs of family members are affixed to lend verisimilitude to painted scenes. Photocopies of documents are appended as proof of the divine intercession. A commercially printed image of the Virgin is glued to a spot on the retablo specially prepared for the purpose. Unlike santos, therefore, Mexican ex-votos have not been threatened with extinction because of the advent of cheap, industrially produced products. On the contrary, the range of techniques available to retablo artists has multiplied and the genre has continued to evolve.

These five conventions are combined in manifold ways to create the form and substance of modern retablos. From an aesthetic point of view, the artistic power of Mexican retablo painting comes from the economy of its execution and the innocent intensity of the emotions it conveys. "The drawing is naively painstaking, the color choices are odd, the perspective is awkward, space is reduced to a rudimentary stage, and action is condensed to highlights. Adherence to appearances is less important than the dramatization of the ghastly event or the miraculous encounter between the victim and the resplendent holy image" (Herrera 1983:151).

In a retablo dealing with illness, "color and drama abound. Women, men, and children are dressed in their best and the sick bed is covered with fringes and swagged drapes. The horizon is often tipped up surrealistically to show the objects in the back to greater advantage, and the characters are often stacked behind each other" (Giffords 1991:49). When the subject is a miraculous delivery from a threatening situation, "the victim is shown in different stages—actively involved in the incident, and passively, as supplicant" (Giffords 1991:49).

Retablos thus condense the most extreme of human emotions—fear, sorrow, apprehension, gratitude, relief, horror—onto small sheets of tin painted in the most elemental of styles. Looking at people depicted in the throes of a circumstance that appears to have no earthly remedy, or facing an imminent personal loss so crushing and painful that all consolation seems hopeless, we not only share the intensity of the fear and sorrow, we also experience the relief of delivery and the unmitigated joy that follow an unbelievable stroke of good luck.

It is the rendering of such powerful and basic human emotions in such simple and unpretentious artistic terms that makes retablos so compelling as works of art. As the folklorist Frances Toor noted in 1947, "*Retablos* or votive offerings are the most important and popular aspect of folk painting at the present time. . . . Many of these *retablos*—realistic pictures of super-realistic events—are painted with great sensitivity and profound recognition of a truth that makes a miracle of reality and of reality a miracle" (1947:67–68).

3
▼▼▼

ARTISTS AND RETABLOS

etablos are generally the commissioned works of untrained popular artists who specialize in such paintings, although at times they may be prepared by the votaries themselves (Herrera 1983:463). Despite the relatively large number of retablos now in museums, galleries, private collections, and churches, however, little is known about the people who actually paint them (Sánchez Lara 1990). Although this lack of information is understandable in the case of santos, whose creators can be assumed to have expired years ago, it is less defensible in the case of ex-votos, because these works continue to be produced today.

Knowing little about *retablistas*, as the artists are called, detracts from a full and complete understanding of the genre, because as Charlot (1949:139) observes, "Anonymity veils the origin of much folk art and allows the sophisticate to make much of the product and little of the producer." In order to shed additional light on retablos and their production, we sought out and interviewed a practicing retablista.

Finding one of these folk artists required some detective work because few sign their works, and even fewer include their address along with their signature. After examining hundreds of retablos in the Church of San Juan de los Lagos, we encountered one painting dated 1969 that included an address in the city of León on the back. (The same address, as it turns out, appeared on a 1972 ex-voto dedicated to el Señor de la Villaseca in Guanajuato [see Romandía de Cantú 1978].) That address led us to Booth 370 of the Aldama Market, and from there to a "known residence" in Rancho San José de Calera, Guanajuato, located in the Municipio of San Francisco del Rincón, about 30 kilometers outside of the city of León. It was there on August 4, 1989, that we met and interviewed Don Vicente Barajas.

Then 73 years old, Don Vicente left his native rancho when he was very young. Migrating to the state of Veracruz, he found work at the Río Blanco textile factory, the scene of several landmark labor disputes leading up to the Mexican Revolution (see Knight 1986:135–51). Although he was first employed in the pressing department, it was later in the electrical plant that he met Don Joaquín Arreola who, in addition to his factory work, painted and decorated fabrics in his spare time.

The two men began working together and Don Vicente slowly learned the intricacies of painting. Together they cut pieces of fabric into one-meter squares and sewed them together to form cushions and table covers. On these items they painted floral designs and sold them in the market each Sunday. After a while, Don Vicente became assistant to another painter and joined him in decorating churches, painting miniatures, and adorning small religious images. Later he worked painting leaves, plants, and flowers on cardboard sheets for a "pharmacist" who used them as advertisements for herbal medicines he hawked in the market.

Although Don Vicente was quite content in Veracruz, bad news from home eventually forced his return. Back on his native rancho in Guanajuato, his liking for drawing and his artistic abilities soon became known, and he began to attract commissions for votive works. Don Guadalupe Rangel, from the nearby rancho of Mezquitillo, was the first to request a retablo—a votive of thanks to the Virgin of San Juan de Los Lagos.

It seems that Don Lupe had been assaulted by bandits on the highway and his horse was wounded. The animal fell several times, and in desperation Don Lupe invoked the holy name of the Virgin. At the last moment, the horse succeeded in standing up and galloping away from the robbers, who were on foot, thereby saving his life. Don Vicente listened carefully to the story and painted a rendition of the miraculous event accompanied by an explanatory text. That day in 1942 when Don Vicente delivered his first painting, he earned three pesos (less than a dollar at the time) and began his career as a retablista.

In 1942, the United States organized the Bracero Program to recruit Mexican laborers for temporary agricultural work north of the border (Galarza 1964; Samora 1971); and like thousands of others from the state of Guanajuato, Don Vicente joined the wave of men moving northward. On March 22, 1945, he obtained Bracero Contract number 129275 and set out for *el norte* for the first time. Over the years, he traveled back and forth to the United States a total of 26 times, performing farm work in the states of Arizona, Michigan, Texas, New Mexico, California, and Nevada.

His trips lasted anywhere from a few months to several years, depending on the work; but always he returned home to his tiny rancho. As a bracero, he combined his talent for art with his new vocation of migrant worker. Art provided a good way of earning extra money on his trips away from home, because during the long train journeys to and from the United States, he could occupy himself by drawing pictures of fellow travelers and selling them for modest fees.

He also continued to paint retablos for migrants who wished to fulfill some vow of thanks to a holy image upon their return. The votive topics typically dealt with work accidents or worries about family members so far away. At this stage in his career, Don Vicente charged $10 per retablo. On his trips to the United States he always bought new tin sheets, paints, and brushes, because he preferred American supplies and materials, especially the brushes.

On one of his return trips to Mexico, he found work as a painter in a hat factory in San Francisco del Rincón. At that time Mexican cowboy hats with painted decorations were in fashion, and there weren't enough people able to paint the intricate designs. After showing the factory owner some samples of his artwork, Don Vicente was hired to paint 60,000 hats stored in a warehouse at 35 cents per hat. He settled in town for a year or two to work for the factory, reserving Sundays to paint religious objects that he sold in the market and at regional fairs.

Don Vicente estimates that over the course of his life he has painted some 5,000 retablos. He still keeps a sign in the Aldama Market and goes into León each day to pick up new requests and deliver the retablos he has completed. His clients are ordinary men and women from the west-central states who seek votives dedicated to the principal icons of the region: el Señor de Villaseca in Guanajuato, la Virgen de Zapopan near Guadalajara, la Virgen de Talpa in Jalisco, el Niño de Atocha in Zacatecas, and el Señor del Saucito in San Luis Potosí. By far the largest number, however, are dedicated to la Virgen de San Juan de los Lagos.

Over the course of 50 years he has prepared votives dedicated to images located in more distant places as well, including Juan Soldado in Tijuana, San Lorenzo in Ciudad Juárez, el Santo Niño de Tepeaca in Puebla, and la Virgen de Guadalupe in Mexico City. He has even received requests by letter, such as the one that arrived from a woman from Guatemala who was assaulted on a highway. Nine shots were fired into the bus on which she was riding, and she emerged unscathed after entrusting herself to el Señor del Saucito in San Luis Potosí. By letter she narrated what happened and indicated the age and sex of the people involved. With these facts, he made a retablo, sent it, and by return mail received a check.

Before making a retablo, Don Vicente asks the patron to tell him the events in detail. He then determines the kind of retablo he needs to paint, charging different prices according to the amount of work and the size of the picture. Retablo scenes involving automobile accidents, horses, or families are the most difficult to execute and the most expensive. The cheapest are the classic scenes of thanksgiving that simply show a person kneeling and praying to a divine image. In 1989, his prices varied from 25,000 to 50,000 pesos per commission (roughly $10 to $20 U.S. dollars).

When a special work is requested, Don Vicente quizzes the client about the facts surrounding the event: the age and sex of the people involved, the color of their skin, the style and color of their clothes, the features of the landscape, and other distinguishing characteristics. He often requests a written version of the text in order to transcribe it exactly. In cases in which clients are unable to supply the words, he must provide them himself, but he warns the client that he does not spell very well. Don Vicente did not go to school, and he learned how to read and write on his own. On only four occasions has he received a complaint about his artistry, however, in each case because the patron felt that his drawing did not represent accurately what really happened.

Don Vicente gets his tin sheets from the hardware store La Palma in León and tempera paints from various paint shops. He buys brushes from a stationery store that carries imported materials because now he prefers those made in Germany. In order to paint on sheet metal, Don Vicente first puts down three or four gray undercoats. Then he distributes the spaces: one area for the image of the Virgin, another for the rendering of the event, and another for the text. He then traces out the areas and draws with a pencil the miraculous occurrence and the theme. Finally he paints in the figures and scenery in vibrant colors. He can usually do one retablo a day, and sometimes two.

When you ask Don Vicente where the people's desire for retablos comes from, he responds, "From faith." He will not pass this vocation on to his children, however. They have become

Jehovah's Witnesses and disapprove of his painting retablos because they believe his paintings make people think more of art than of God. Although they do not want him to paint anymore, he continues to ply his vocation when they are not around and privately he remains a Catholic.

Although Don Vicente clearly falls in the category of a folk artist, the line between the inexpert hand of the amateur and the skilled hand of the master is not always so clear, and at least one critically acclaimed painter began his career as a retablista. The nineteenth-century artist Hermenegildo Bustos has come to be widely admired by later generations of Mexican artists (see Fernández 1952; Aceves Barajas 1956; Tibol 1983; Paz 1988), and he has been especially influential among Mexican realist painters (Ramírez 1990). Four of his works were included in the retrospective exhibition *Mexico: Splendors of Thirty Centuries* (Metropolitan Museum of Art, 1990).

Many of Bustos's surviving paintings consist of votive works prepared for friends and neighbors who had commissioned them to give thanks to local icons, such as el Señor de la Columna in his home town of Purísima del Rincón, Guanajuato (Aceves Barajas 1956; Sánchez Lara 1990). Given the posthumous recognition of Bustos's talent and the later regard in which his paintings came to be held, an unusual number of his retablos, which were originally painted without signature, have been identified, preserved, and dated. The oldest surviving votive work attributed to Hermenegildo Bustos dates from 1852, when the painter was only 20 years old (Aceves Barajas 1956:58), and the last was finished in 1906, just before his death the following year (Westheim 1951:11).

Over the course of 50 years of painting, Bustos played a major role in preserving and transmitting the popular culture of his native region of Rincón, Guanajuato. In addition to painting theatrical and liturgical representations, he created a permanent register of the region's life and times, a kind of diary that captured and interpreted its anecdotes, customs, happenings, and events. A total of 67 of his retablos have been identified, most of which are in private collections (such as those of Aceves Barajas, Orozco Muñoz, del Valle Prieto, Piña, Durand-Arias, and Rionda Arreguín). Many of these retablos have been exhibited in shows put together in 1951 at the Palacio de Bellas Artes in Mexico City; in 1992 at the Museum of la Alhóndiga de Granaditas in Guanajuato; in 1992 at the exposition of the Cremi Cultural Foundation in Guadalajara; and in 1993 at the National Museum of Art in Mexico City.

One Bustos retablo from the Cremi Cultural exhibit tells the story of a U.S. migrant, Don Ruperto Herrera, who was on his way north in 1906 when an electric train carrying earth and stone derailed, tipped over, and trapped many people underneath its great weight. Although 14 people perished in the accident, the supplicant survived with just a broken leg because "he didn't cease to invoke the Holiest Lord of the Column, being well cured in little time" (Ruy Sánchez 1992).

Another influential artist of the pre-revolutionary era was not himself a retablista but, none-theless, admired retablos and drew inspiration from the votive tradition. José Guadalupe Posada (Fernández 1952; Rivera 1958) is best known today for his engravings of skeletons from Mexico's Day of the Dead celebration and for his political caricatures of the Porfirian elite, but on several occasions he created works fashioned after ex-votos.

From his earliest days in Aguascalientes, Posada worked to support himself as an illustrator for local newspapers. When he arrived in Mexico City and began his artistic career at the print studio of Venegas Arroyo, he continued to earn extra money by illustrating newspapers, some of which were of a satiric nature, such as *El Hijo de Ahuizote*, edited by the brothers Flores Magón (Díaz de León 1985). Through his illustrations Posada, like Bustos, was able to represent his epoch and its people. He was the first artist, however, to incorporate the formal structure of the retablo into his work, which was in another medium entirely.

Posada used the retablo format to illustrate "miraculous" events and exceptional happenings for common people to read about in flyers and tabloids. One of his illustrations accompanied an article about a house on fire; it showed a blaze erupting from a hearth located to the right of an interior scene. As the fire threatens a young boy, his father attempts to put it out with a seltzer bottle while the mother falls on her knees to pray to the Virgin of Guadalupe, who appears suspended in clouds in the upper left-hand corner of the frame (Berdecio and Appelbaum 1972). In another engraving, the Virgin appears suspended in clouds above the sickbed of a woman surrounded by family members and onlookers (Posada 1930). In yet another print, Christ appears suspended in clouds as a man plummets toward earth during an accident in a hot-air balloon (Berdecio and Appelbaum 1972).

Despite the influence of retablos on the work of popular artists like Bustos and Posada, it was not until the era of the Mexican Revolution that painted ex-votos came to the notice of Mexico's fine artists and moved out of cheap newspapers and curio shops and into museums and private collections. Many of Mexico's greatest artists of the twentieth century collected retablos, drew inspiration from them in their work, and discussed their merits in their writings.

Perhaps the first to draw inspiration from the votive tradition was Angel Zárraga, an early modernist painter (Fernández 1983). In 1910 he painted a work on canvas entitled *Ex-voto San Sebastián y Adorante* that paid special homage to the Mexican retablo. The painting shows a woman dressed in black and praying before an image of Saint Sebastian. To the side of the picture, in a special area a text states: "Lord, I don't know how to worship you like a poet, with complicated verses, but accept this crude and humble work that I have made with my mortal hands. Angel Zárraga."

Although the text, image, and kneeling supplicant replicate the essential features of the Mexican ex-voto, a modernist play on identity lies in the fact that the supplicant is a woman and not the man Zárraga, who signs the accompanying text, and that Zárraga's own face is substituted for Saint Sebastian's. Thus, by painting an ironic retablo to the holy image, Zárraga identifies the votive act with his life and calling as a painter, seeing it as a form of martyrdom to art (Fernández 1983).

Roberto Montenegro was also impressed with the aesthetic possibilities of retablos, although he did not use them directly in his own work. He wrote that retablos "are imbued with the characteristics of the miracles they represent, and through their fine plastic feeling they become real masterpieces" (Montenegro 1950:12). In his classic treatise on Mexican painting, he explained their artistic appeal in this way: "The lack of technique, the discretion in the use of tones and the inimitable charm of the fashion of the time . . . makes [*sic*] us see in those old and timeworn portraits the qualities which by their own merit, obliges [*sic*] us to give them a place of preference in our admiration" (Montenegro 1934:15–16).

It was Montenegro who, together with fellow artist Jorge Enciso, put together the Exposition of Popular Art in 1921, the first full-scale show of folk art in Mexican history. Supported and financed by the revolutionary government of President Alvaro Obregón, the exhibition explicitly intended to introduce popular Mexican traditions to a wider, more "cultured" public, and to elevate these authentic expressions of the Mexican spirit to the status of fine arts (Martínez Peñaloza 1988). Since then, Mexican retablos have been exhibited many times, most recently in the show *Mexico: Splendors of Thirty Centuries* at New York's Metropolitan Museum of Art (1990).

The catalog of the 1921 exposition was written by Gerardo Murillo, better known as Dr. Atl, and in volume two of *Las Artes Populares en Mexico* (1922) he presented ten retablos drawn largely from the state of Tlaxcala from the years 1890 through 1920. In introducing the paintings, Dr. Atl wrote that "ex-votos, known generally as retablos, are . . . pictorial works of great interest for their incredible innocence and because they represent, more than any other manifestation, the popular faith [of Mexico]" (Atl 1922:91–92).

Retablos also interested the great revolutionary muralist David Alfaro Siqueiros, who reports having seen them as a child with his father, a fervent Catholic. Years later, in 1917, as an atheist officer in the revolutionary army of General Venustiano Carranza, he sought "to go to see some retablos in the town of Guadalupe, popular religious objects that I had learned to enjoy in childhood. . . . [After] looking at these pictures for a long time, and also reading their marvelous stories, I noted that nearby on a piece of cloth were many retablos thrown on the floor, making a true mountain, along with broken candelabras and other typical church adornments." There he found one made of paper and "painted with colored pencils, but especially interesting, perhaps more primitive than the others, almost as if executed by a child. And thinking that I was not doing anything wrong, I picked it up for myself."

At this moment, a priest entered and shouted at him, "You are a thief!" Siqueiros tried to defend himself, insisting that the retablos were thrown out and abandoned, and that it didn't seem wrong to rescue one, especially because he himself was a painter. But his explanations were useless. The priest continued shouting "Thief!" until a pair of sacristans came to his aid. On trying to leave, Siqueiros pushed the priest aside, but the cleric took out a "lady's pistol" from under his cassock while the sacristans took out theirs, forming an armed row. Siqueiros, who was also armed with a regulation .45, dug in with his own pistol. Three policemen, also armed, finally showed up to stave off the possibility of a firefight, but the dispute continued to the police station (Siqueiros 1977:76).

Diego Rivera, unschooled in the manners of the Revolution, also admired retablos but preferred to buy retablos instead of "stealing" them from churches. Over the course of his life, he came to own a great many of these paintings, which are still exhibited at the home he shared with Frida Kahlo in Coyoacán, now a museum open to the public (Tibol 1986). According to Rivera, "the anguish of our people caused this strange flowering of painted ex-votos to rise up slowly against the walls of their churches" (quoted in Charlot 1949:142).

Rivera believed that Mexico's mestizo culture gave rise to two important artistic expressions: retablos and murals in *pulquerías* (places serving *pulque*, an alcoholic brew made from the maguey cactus). With his usual nationalist and Marxist bombast, he averred that churches and pulquerías "are the only places that the bourgeoisie has left in plain possession of the people, because taverns and churches serve exactly the same function, since alcohol and religion are both good sedatives and efficacious anesthetics, ensuring that the proletarian masses don't feel their hunger and pain so strongly that they make whimsical demands or unexpectedly form subversive organizations" (Rivera 1979:67).

For Rivera, the native Mexican genius flowed from pulque and religion: "Everything else falls apart and becomes contaminated; but in the end, the tremendous vitality of the Mexican people will transform vile influences into works of art. . . ." Thus retablos were "a product where the esthetics of Europe, imposed on Mexican painters by the invading Spanish, were digested to give birth to a mestizo product, but one reflecting a positive, vital, and therefore happy mixture, capable of persisting through time and space and preserving intact its popular identity" (Rivera 1979:57).

On at least one occasion, Rivera put his admiration of retablos into practice. When during the 1920s the labor leader Vicente Lombardo Toledano wanted to prepare a pamphlet to counter the admonition of conservative priests that land redistribution was against the teachings of Christ, Diego Rivera, the good communist, offered his services to create an illustration for the cover: an engraving drawn in the manner of a retablo.

The picture shows a poor campesino plowing his land behind two oxen while the peasant's wife sits nearby with tortillas and a basket. In the upper right corner of the print, Christ appears suspended in clouds with his sacred heart exposed, and the text states: "El reparto de tierras a los pobres no se opone a las enseñanzas de Nuestro Señor Jesucristo y de la Santa Madre Iglesia. El pueblo mexicano peleó y sufrió diez años queriendo hallar la palabra de Nuestro Señor Jesucristo" (The redistribution of lands to the poor is not against the teachings of Jesus Christ or the Holy Mother Church. The Mexican people fought and suffered for ten years seeking to find the word of Our Lord Jesus) (Charlot 1963:25; Tibol 1986). The religious image, text, composition, and placement of the figures clearly mark the work as a retablo.

Rivera's student and collaborator in the muralist movement, Jean Charlot, saw the power of retablos as emanating from their expression of the duality between the human and the divine. "Like the scaffold-sets of medieval mystery plays, the plastic dramas of the retablos are tiered vertically. Man is a kind of deep-air animal crawling on rock bottom, his face lifted to a stratosphere where the holy beings dwell. These in turn bend over the ledge of the dense pool, in search of their faithful" (Charlot 1949:141).

Despite the concrete and extensive evidence of retablos' importance to Posada, Zárraga, Montenegro, Atl, Siqueiros, Rivera, and Charlot, the artist who was most profoundly influenced by the genre was clearly Frida Kahlo (Garduño Pulido 1990; Lowe 1991:48). The influence of retablos is evident in several aspects of her work, the most obvious being her predilection for sheet metal as an artistic medium. Of the 76 works presented in Zamora's (1990) catalog, 16 percent were on metal and 40 percent were on masonite, another common retablo medium; another 7 percent were executed on wood and 8 percent were rendered on paper or cardboard. In all, only 30 percent of her works were on canvas, the painter's traditional medium.

A second indication of the retablo influence on Kahlo's work was the relatively small size of her paintings. Retablos generally range in size from 9 to 280 square inches, with 140 square inches being typical (Giffords 1991:37–38). The paintings included in Zamora's (1990) catalog average about 360 square inches (roughly 1.5 feet square), which is slightly larger than the maximum for retablos; but 44 percent of Kahlo's works fall below this size, and about one-fifth have dimensions approximately equal to those of the typical retablo.

Finally, the influence of retablos is evident in the compositional structure and style of many of Kahlo's paintings—the deliberate use of naive primitivism, the frequent inclusion of floating images and apparitions, and the recurrent incorporation of explanatory texts. According to Kahlo's biographer, "Retablos form the single most important source for Frida's primitivizing style, and even as her paintings become less primitive and more realistic, retablos continued to be a principal model" (Herrera 1983:151). One curator has noted that "after 1932 retablos for Frida constituted the most important source for her style" (Garduño Pulido 1990:7).

Some of Frida Kahlo's best-known works are, in fact, little more than retablos in their purest form. *The Henry Ford Hospital* (1932), for example, was Frida's first effort in the retablo style (Garduño Pulido 1990). It was painted in Detroit, where Diego Rivera (her husband) had been commissioned by the Ford family to create a mural at the Detroit Institute of Fine Arts (Herrera 1983).

During her stay in Michigan, Kahlo suffered a traumatic miscarriage. Her rendition of the event shows her lying on a bloody hospital bed that is located on a featureless olive-colored plane, which extends back to a stark industrial skyline of factories, smokestacks, and water towers silhouetted against a blue sky filled with wispy clouds. Floating around the bed are symbolic images connected to Frida's belly with red ribbons, and on the bedframe a short text gives the date and location.

This painting very clearly employs several common elements of retablo painting: clouds, floating images, text, a surreal perspective, a single event isolated in time and space, a minimalist background. As in popular retablos, these devices are disarmingly effective in capturing the psychological pain of loss. In its depiction of a solitary hospital bed against a bleak and lifeless background, the composition is strikingly similar to retablos prepared by U.S. migrants who have fallen ill while in the United States (see fig. 22 for an example).

A Few Small Nips (1935) was inspired by a newspaper story about a drunken man who threw his wife on a cot and then stabbed her 20 times; when he appeared before the judge he protested that he had only given her "a few small nips." Although thematically the painting is closely connected to the prints of José Guadalupe Posada, it is clearly executed in the style of a retablo (Herrera 1983:188). Painted on metal, its small size of 181 square inches (11.6 × 15.6) falls well within the range typical of the genre. The perspective is awkward and the drawing is intentionally primitive and expressionless.

In her rendition of the ghastly event, Kahlo has stripped the scene to its essentials. In a bare room with a pale green floor, white walls, and a blue strip around the baseline, the mutilated and bloody corpse of a naked woman sprawls on a crude bed that is drawn out of perspective. The white sheets and pillow upon which the body lies are splotched crimson, and standing above the cot is a man with one hand in his pocket and the other holding a bloody knife. He wears a fedora and a white shirt covered with blood stains. He appears detached; his posture is casual, and his crudely drawn face reveals little emotion. Above the gruesome scene two doves carry a ribbon with the words *Unos Cuantos Piquetitos* (A Few Small Nips).

As if she were a retablista commissioned to record the sad affair, Kahlo faithfully employs the structure and composition of a retablo—in her juxtaposition of contrasting colors, her rendering of awkward perspective, her use of text, her employment of floating images, her depiction of human experience in extremis, and in her generally spare treatment of a powerfully emotional scene. The man standing next to the deathbed of his wife is a deliberately ironic play on the common retablo scene of anxious family members lined up next to a sickbed (indeed, a preliminary sketch of the work also had a child standing by the bed [see Zamora 1990:51]).

Frida Kahlo's appropriation of the technique and role of the retablo painter went even further than these suggestive examples. While on a visit to the United States in 1939, she was commissioned by the wealthy socialite Clare Boothe Luce to paint a portrait of Dorothy Hale, a failed starlet who was an acquaintance of both women and who had recently committed suicide by jumping from an upper floor of the Hampshire House Hotel in New York City.

In discharging the commission, Frida adopted outright the role of the retablo painter and the "portrait" is very patently a retablo. Most of the frame is taken up by a rendering of the Hampshire House viewed through a mass of swirling clouds that have parted near an upper floor to reveal a tiny figure jumping from a window. Halfway down the building a much larger figure is seen plummeting headfirst toward earth, with arms and legs askew; in the foreground a large figure lies inert in an empty brown, featureless space wearing a black velvet evening gown and a yellow corsage.

The dead starlet is very beautiful, and although blood drips from her ears and mouth, her countenance is composed and her eyes stare directly at the viewer. At the base of the painting a short text appears in blood red: "En la ciudad de Nueva York el día 21 del mes de OCTUBRE de 1938, a las seis de la mañana, se suicidó la señora DOROTHY HALE tirándose desde una ventana muy alta del edificio Hampshire House. En su recuerdo, Clare Boothe Luce pidió para la madre de Dorothy este retablo, habiéndolo ejecutado, FRIDA KAHLO." (In the City of New York on the 21st of the month of OCTOBER, 1938, at six in the morning, Mrs. DOROTHY HALE committed suicide by throwing herself out of a very high window of the Hampshire House. In her memory,

Clare Boothe Luce requested for the mother of Dorothy this retablo, having executed it, FRIDA KAHLO [Herrera 1983:293].)

Almost all the elements of the classic Mexican retablo are captured in this celebrated work of art: a bleak, surreal use of space; the segmentation of time and the condensation of action to highlights (the three phases of the fall); the depiction of images in clouds; the use of bold contrasting colors; the provision of an explanatory text written in childlike grammar; a script that mixes capital and small letters; a deliberate blurring of the border between life and death (dripping blood and an inert body with a composed and beautiful countenance making eye contact with the viewer).

Not being familiar with the Mexican retablo genre, however, Mrs. Luce was horrified by the picture and nearly had it destroyed. She only agreed to preserve it if the phrase "Clare Boothe Luce requested for the mother of Dorothy" were painted out, and to this day a noticeable gap remains in the retablo's text. Despite her unfortunate experience with Mrs. Luce, however, Frida Kahlo continued to borrow stylistic elements and techniques from retablo painting to the end of her life.

An intriguing conundrum in Mexican art history is why the leading artists of the twentieth century showed such intense interest in ex-votos but displayed such limited enthusiasm for santos. Both genres constitute folk paintings on tin, both are religious in nature, and both came of age and enjoyed a surge in popularity at about the same time (the late nineteenth century). Yet Giffords is "surprised by the absence of references to the paintings of saints on tin in sources by writers who prided themselves on their appreciation of popular folk art. Although Dr. Atl, Anita Brenner, Gabriel Fernández Ledesma, Roberto Montenegro, Frida Kahlo, and Diego Rivera have praised or collected the *retablo ex-voto* and perhaps even found inspiration in the art form, the *retablo santo* is virtually ignored" (Giffords 1991:58).

To gain an understanding of this paradox, one must begin with the Mexican Revolution of 1910, which transformed the social order of the country and brought to power a mestizo class that had long chafed under the yoke of criollo domination (Hansen 1971; Hart 1987; Knight 1986). In the years leading up to 1910, elites under the dictator Porfirio Díaz had looked down on Indians, glorified European culture, and deprecated the mixture of European and Indian bloods. The Revolution's victors, in contrast, exalted Mexico's Indian heritage, lauded the accomplishments of pre-Columbian civilizations, and saw the mixture of the European and Indian bloods not as a source of shame, but as a new source of pride (see Vasconcelos 1926; Paz 1961; Ramos 1962). In this process of ideological transformation, the Catholic Church generally played a conservative role, opposing change and defending the status quo (Knight 1986; Hart 1987).

Against this backdrop, santos proved unattractive to the radical young artists seeking to establish a new, dynamic, and distinctively Mexican art. Painted santos had been brought into Mexico by priests in order to evangelize the Indians and cultivate Catholic fervor. To the anti-clerical artists of the Revolution, therefore, they bore the taint of the old regime. This association with the former rulers was reinforced by the fact that most patrons of santos were wealthy criollos. Although the art form had spread to other classes by the late Porfiriato, it occurred just as santos were being replaced by industrially produced products and their adoption by the masses was never complete. In addition, rather than providing a model for a new and distinctively "Mexican" art, santos represented little more than rigid copies of European icons. Finally, whereas artists such as Rivera, Siqueiros, and Orozco sought to create a public art that would disseminate the ideals of the Revolution, santos were a private genre whose essential purpose lay in the inspiration of devotion within the confines of the home.

The very nature of santos, therefore, rendered them politically suspect and intrinsically un-suited to the artistic aspirations of the artists emerging from the Mexican Revolution. Rather than providing a model for a new art that was public, mestizo, and popular, santos constituted a genre that was private, criollo, and bourgeois. Ex-votos, in contrast, fit the needs of the Revolution perfectly.

Although both genres grew out of religious altar painting, ex-votos ultimately had deeper, more popular roots in the votive cultures of ancient Mesoamerica and pagan Europe. Ex-votos thus embodied the ideal of *mestizaje*, or mixture, promoted by the Revolution. In addition, the subjects of ex-votos were not Church-approved icons of European origin, but the everyday experiences of ordinary Mexicans; and unlike santos, ex-votos had been fully embraced by the masses by the time of the Revolution. (Indeed, as Dr. Atl [1922:92–93] pointed out, during the worst of the violence retablos were assiduously sought and jealously preserved by troops sacking and destroying Mexico's churches.) Finally, as paintings explicitly intended for public display, ex-votos provided an alluring model for muralists seeking to create a new public art.

Not only did ex-votos have desirable social attributes, they also had appealing artistic properties. Whereas santos arose from a static idiom that discouraged innovation and required the duplication of approved images, ex-votos set only the broadest parameters on style and allowed great latitude for individual interpretation and creativity. Whereas santos were painted in subdued colors following rigid compositional rules, ex-votos were rendered in a range of colors subject to only the broadest of artistic guidelines. It is not surprising, therefore, that ex-votos were admired by Mexico's post-Revolutionary artists and deeply influenced their work, whereas santos died out in the 1920s and had little lasting effect on the development of Mexican fine arts and aesthetics.

4

▼▼▼

SACRED SHRINES, HOLY ICONS, AND MIGRANTS

Veneration of holy images is a popular and ancient tradition in Mexico going back to before the Conquest (Lafaye 1976). The country's best-known icon is, of course, the Virgin of Guadalupe, the patroness of the nation and "the Queen of Mexico," who in 1531 appeared to Juan Diego, a newly converted Amerindian of humble origin, on the hill of Tepeyac just outside of Mexico City, where the Virgin's Basilica now stands (Genaro Cuadriello 1989). Each region in Mexico has its own venerated figure, however, and the states of Jalisco, Guanajuato, and San Luis Potosí, long noted for the intensity of their faith and devotion (see Meyer, 1976), are replete with their own images of Christ and the Virgin.

In Europe, votive activity traditionally focused on saints and their relics. The New World, of course, had no indigenous saints in the years immediately following the Conquest, and the relics that did find their way into the Americas remained largely in cathedrals and monasteries, where they were reserved for the contemplation of the elite; they were not placed in regional churches or local shrines for the spiritual benefit of the masses (Sánchez Lara 1990). The religious fervor generated by mass evangelization during the colonial period demanded popular outlets, however (Giffords 1974:19–20).

In Mexico, this need for objects of popular devotion was met not by saints' relics, but by sacred images of Christ and the Virgin. Often of local manufacture and idiosyncratic in design and execution, these images gradually came to be imbued with miraculous powers in the minds of the people. Over the years, an oral tradition of legends and testimony arose to affirm a popular lore of divine interventions and miraculous happenings, and ultimately the images themselves became objects of votive supplication.

Out of the hundreds of icons scattered in sanctuaries large and small throughout Mexico, we chose to examine votive works associated with eight particular images: four of the crucified Christ, one of the child Jesus, and three of the Virgin Mary. These images were selected because their shrines all lie within a few hours' drive of Mexico's leading migrant-sending communities, which are scattered throughout the states of Guanajuato, Jalisco, Michoacán, Nayarit, San Luis Potosí, and Zacatecas (see map, opposite).

Together these states make up the region in Mexico from which the greatest number of migrants hail (Gamio 1930; Samora 1971; Dagodag 1975; North and Houstoun 1976; Ranney and Kossoudji 1983), and the eight images together constitute the most important shrines in the area. Each site has a long history of votive supplication by U.S. migrants, so that by focusing on these eight images we ensure sufficient material for a detailed analysis of migrants' retablos. Votive paintings commissioned or painted by migrants can be viewed in the sanctuaries themselves or obtained through private galleries that specialize in Mexican popular arts.

Images of Christ
El Señor de Villaseca

The sanctuary of el Señor de Villaseca is located near Mineral de Cata, a silver mine situated on the outskirts of the city of Guanajuato. Mining operations began there shortly after the city's founding in 1557, and a small settlement arose around the mine's entrance. According to local legend, el Señor de Villaseca was brought from Spain in 1618 by its proprietor, a wealthy hacienda owner named Don Alonso de Villaseca. A sanctuary was constructed to house the image in 1725 and rebuilt to new specifications in 1788. The church is composed of a bell tower that rises grace-

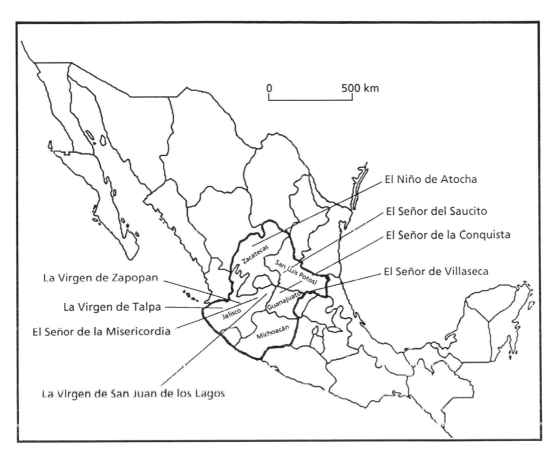

El Niño de Atocha

El Señor del Saucito

El Señor de la Conquista

El Señor de Villaseca

La Virgen de Zapopan

La Virgen de Talpa

El Señor de la Misericordia

La Virgen de San Juan de los Lagos

Zacatecas

San Luis Potosí

Jalisco

Guanajuato

Michoacán

The states of western Mexico and the location of key shrines in Guanajuato, Jalisco, Zacatecas, and San Luis Potosí.

fully from a facade of ornate columns and friezes sculpted in the Mexican churrigueresque style (Sánchez Lara 1990).

The image of el Señor de Villaseca, also known as el Cristo Negro (the Black Christ) because of its tawny color, is located on the sanctuary's principal altar. Christ is depicted wounded and nailed to the cross; a red cloth with gold trim covers his loins and a crown of thorns draws blood from his head, which falls lifelessly against his right shoulder. Rays of golden light emanate from the center of the cross, and the top of the vertical beam is capped with a golden ornament stamped INRI (the Latin acronym for Iesus Nazarenus, Rex Iudaeorum—Jesus of Nazareth, King of the Jews).

Despite the image's legendary origins, it is doubtful that it was actually brought from Spain by Don Alonso de Villaseca. Rather, its materials and style of construction point to a Mexican origin sometime during the sixteenth century. The image was sculpted from a spongy paste known as *tiazinquis*, a mixture of corn pith and the juice of orchid bulbs, which was molded over a frame of dried cornstalks (Sánchez Lara 1990:58). After drying, the paste was covered with a layer of plaster made from chalk and oil, which was in turn covered with a film that yielded a smooth surface ready for painting (Sánchez Lara 1990:58). The final coat was a tree sap that hardened to preserve the image (Carrillo y Gariel 1949; Giffords 1974:57).

Before the Conquest, the technique of *titzingueni* was used by the Tarascan Amerindians of Michoacán to create images of their gods. Early in the sixteenth century, however, the craft was turned to Christian uses by Bishop Vasco de Quiroga, the benevolent missionary posted to the Tarascan capital of Tzintzuntzan in 1523. Seeking to preserve the skills of native artisans and give them a useful vocation, Bishop Quiroga encouraged the craft of titzingueni but put its practitioners to work making Christian images instead of Tarascan icons (Giffords 1974:57). Over time, the holy images produced by the Tarascans acquired a reputation for their high quality and fine workmanship and were widely distributed throughout colonial Mexico; a few even reached sanctuaries in Spain (Sánchez Lara 1990).

El Señor de Villaseca was thus probably created by Tarascan Amerindians working under Vasco de Quiroga in the latter half of the sixteenthth century. Although it is unclear when the image began to attract votaries, the Museum of the Alhóndiga in Guanajuato contains one retablo dated 1822 in which a woman gives thanks to el Señor de Villaseca for saving her husband from execution during the War of Independence (1810–20).

The earliest documented ex-voto dedicated to this image comes from the memoirs of a sacristan who served in the sanctuary shortly after the War of Independence. Among the many retablos he reported seeing during his service, one particularly struck his fancy: a picture of a young woman, carrying a basket covered with cloth, who was being followed by a darkly cloaked man with a dagger. The man was using the dagger to lift up the cloth to reveal a bouquet of flowers underneath (Almanza Carranza 1981). Although the original work has not been preserved, it was probably left in the late 1700s or early 1800s.

The story behind the retablo is as follows: the woman in question was having a love affair with another man, a miner, while her husband was in jail for some minor infraction. Each morning she brought her lover a basket of food at the mine where he worked. When her husband heard rumors of his wife's infidelity, he became jealous and decided to confront her when he was released from jail.

On the morning following his release, he waited secretly with a dagger by the path she took to the mine. As she walked toward him he surprised her and asked what was in the basket. In a panic she said, "Flowers for el Señor de Villaseca." Not believing her, he lifted the cloth with the dagger and much to the surprise of both uncovered a bouquet of flowers. The next day the woman's lover was found stabbed to death in the mine, but the woman herself was never harmed. A few days later a retablo appeared in the sanctuary showing a young woman and a basket of flowers with a text that offered thanks to el Señor de Villaseca for a great miracle that had been bestowed (Almanza Carranza 1981; Sánchez Lara 1990).

El Señor de la Conquista

Less is known about the origin of el Señor de la Conquista, located in the city of San Felipe Torres Mochas in northern Guanajuato. The icon, known locally as el Señor de los Milagros (The Lord of Miracles), was named to commemorate the "spiritual conquest" of the Amerindians during the sixteenth century. Although the exact date of its creation is unknown, historical references suggest it was installed in the sanctuary by 1585 and was brought to the city from San Miguel de Allende, where another copy of the same image was also deposited (and exists today). For ten years in the late eighteenth century, the figure was under the care and supervision of Miguel Hidalgo, the father of Mexican Independence, who served for a time as a parish priest in San Felipe.

Although the image may have been brought from San Miguel de Allende, its style and method of manufacture once again suggest Tarascan origins in the sixteenth century. Like el Señor de la Villaseca, the image was created from a mixture of corn pith and orchid juice using the technique of titzingueni. As before, Christ is depicted crucified on the cross with his head reclining against the right shoulder. The figure is adorned with a wig of human hair and a white loincloth. The dark yellow flesh shines with a thick coat of lacquer, and although Christ is not wearing a crown of thorns, the body is stained with blood.

It is not clear from available documents when the image first became established as an object of veneration. The earliest retablos we found date from the early twentieth century, but votive supplication of el Señor de la Conquista probably has a more ancient history. Like the image of el Señor de Villaseca, which was created at about the same time, it probably goes back at least to the early nineteenth century, and possibly before.

El Señor del Saucito

The image of el Señor del Saucito has more recent origins than either of the foregoing icons, both of whom share a connection to Mexico's pre-Hispanic past through their Tarascan manufacture. The story of el Señor del Saucito begins in 1820 at a crossroads settlement called Las Encinillas, located about four kilometers from the center of San Luis Potosí. In that year a carpenter of modest means, Cesáreo de la Cruz, came upon a willow trunk with two branches that reminded him of a crucifix (the word *saucito* translates roughly as "little willow"). He thereupon commissioned an Indian craftsman, Juan Pablo, from a neighboring town to carve an image of the crucified Christ from the trunk, and when it was completed Cesáreo placed it on an adobe pedestal, covered it with a bower of fresh branches, and had it blessed by Father Clemente Luna (Alvarez 1987).

Within a few years, the image began to attract pilgrims and votaries from the city and surrounding rural settlements. In 1826, a professional sculptor, José María Aguado, was hired to rework the image and smooth over its imperfections, giving the icon its present form. In that year el Señor del Saucito was placed inside a small chapel, which subsequently was enlarged in 1864 and 1866 to accommodate the ever-growing crowds (Alvarez 1987).

Eventually even these enlargements proved insufficient and the building could no longer contain all the supplicants who came to pay their respects to the wooden image of Christ on the first Friday in March, the icon's annual fiesta day. In 1880 construction began on the present sanctuary. Although the sacristy was finished ten years later, allowing the image to be placed on its present altar, work on the rest of the church languished and was suspended several times for lack of funds and because of civil turmoil. The church was not fully completed until 1954, when the architect Federico Mariscal was hired by the Archbishop of San Luis Potosí to supervise the last phases of construction (Alvarez 1987).

The image itself stands about 5½ feet tall and has a width of roughly five feet from hand to hand. The cross is a little over eight feet tall, fashioned with nails of gold-plated silver and capped with the inscription INRI. On either side of the image are golden suns, angels, and an adornment of branches that symbolize the willow from which the icon was created. Golden rays emanate from Christ's head, which supports a three-peaked crown of gold. A silk cloth with white trim girds the image's loins, and two serpent eggs rest at its feet, a gift from a thankful pilgrim (Alvarez 1987).

El Señor de la Misericordia

Like el Señor del Saucito, el Señor de la Misericordia was fashioned from a tree trunk early in the nineteenth century. The history of this image begins on September 6, 1839, in the rural town of Tepatitlán, Jalisco, when a poor farmer, Don Pedro Medina, saw a strange light emanating from a gully near his home (Casillas 1989). Thinking that a neighbor was making charcoal, he approached the glow only to find an oak tree seeming to offer itself to him as a crucifix. In an emotional state, he returned home, borrowed some oxen, and asked his neighbor, Gerónimo Gómez, to come and help him cut down the tree to create a holy image of Christ.

Don Gerónimo agreed, but on his way he fell ill with a sharp pain in the stomach. Don Pedro ran ahead, cut a splinter from the mysterious oak, and returned to feed it to Don Gerónimo, who suddenly and miraculously recovered his health. Refusing any further assistance, Don Gerónimo cut down the tree all by himself, an event the two men considered miraculous.

Together Don Pedro and Don Gerónimo trimmed the trunk down to a size that could be used to fashion a crucifix. After lashing it to a brace of oxen in order to drag it back to Don Pedro's home, they found it would not move. Then Don Pedro noticed that part of the trunk formed a natural figure of the crucified Christ and that this surface had been turned toward the ground. When they rolled the trunk over, the oxen immediately moved forward and the men felt they had witnessed a second miracle.

When they arrived at Don Pedro's home, the two men left the oak leaning against a wall in the corner of the patio, but later a storm arose and Don Pedro rounded up six neighbors to move it indoors. Once again, they were unable to budge it and it remained outside all night in the wind and rain. The following morning Don Pedro got on his knees and prayed to God that he might carry the mysterious wood indoors to protect it from the elements. Getting up from his prayers, he went out to the patio and immediately lifted the oak onto his shoulders and carried it inside by himself, leaving him convinced that he had participated in yet another miracle.

Within a few days an itinerant wood carver appeared in town, and Don Pedro commissioned him to create the crucifix. Little work was involved because the outlines of a figure of Christ appeared in the wood; the only thing the wood carver had to do was add a crossbeam and a little extra wood for the eyes. For his labors, the sculptor was paid 40 pesos plus an additional 20 in expenses (Casillas 1989).

The image of el Señor de la Misericordia depicts Christ just after the moment of death. Wearing a crown of thorns and nailed to the cross, he has been pierced through the side with a lance. Blood falls from his forehead and spatters on his shoulders and gushes from the open wound in his side. The figure's head leans forward onto the right shoulder and its eyes are closed. It is clad in a red loincloth embroidered with gold leaves and secured with a large sash of the same colors fastened on the right side.

Little more is recorded about the miraculous image until 1852, when on April 28, during the celebration of Saint Peter the Martyr, it was installed in a new sanctuary built expressly to house it. On the following day, the new church opened its doors to receive the adulation of the public and to admit pilgrims from surrounding towns and villages. By this time, apparently, the figure was known for its miraculous powers and retablos had begun to accumulate (Casillas 1989).

Within a few years, the sanctuary proved to be too small to hold the adoring crowds that surged into it every April 28, so the image was removed and paraded through the streets. Typically it spent the night of the 28th in a small parish church before being returned to the main sanctuary on the 29th. After the outbreak of the Revolution in 1910, civil turmoil compelled church authorities to remove the image from its altar for a time and hide it for safekeeping (Casillas 1989).

Since 1943, the procession of the image has become an annual event in Tepatitlán; it is announced at 3:00 P.M. on the Sunday preceding April 28th by the ringing of all the church bells in the city. The procession for el Señor de la Misericordia now includes floats, artistic decorations, military bands, and an escort of mounted *charros* (Mexican cowboys in dark costumes richly embroidered with silver). A river of faithful pilgrims follows the image as it makes its way from parish to parish through the narrow streets of the community, now a city of some 100,000 inhabitants.

El Niño de Atocha

El Niño de Atocha provides a convenient transition to the ensuing discussion of Marian images, because it is the only figure of Christ as a child that we consider, and it is closely connected to a well-known image of the Virgin, Nuestra Señora de Atocha. According to Giffords (1974:50), Nuestra Señora de Atocha "is always seen on retablos with the Child in her arms, for without him in his distinctive costume she would be unidentifiable." In contrast, el Niño has come to stand alone as an independent icon, and in Mexico the adulation paid to him now surpasses that focused on his mother.

Tradition holds that the original image of el Niño was fashioned by Saint Luke and brought to Spain by a patriarch of the Antioch Christian Community during the late Roman Empire. There it was placed in a modest hermitage located in a field of esparto grass, or *atochales*, which give the town of Atocha its name. The hermitage was destroyed during the Moorish invasion of the eighth century, but in 1162 the image reappeared in the Church of Santa Leocadia in Toledo (Giffords 1974).

The Virgin and Child began to acquire separate identities during the time of the Saracen occupation, when the Islamic conquest of the Iberian Peninsula produced a host of Christian captives languishing in Moorish prisons. According to legend, the Moors forbade all visits of mercy except by children, who were only allowed to bring food and water to their starving relatives. "One day a child dressed as a pilgrim came to the prison carrying a basket, a staff, and a gourd of water"; and in a variation of the gospel story of the fishes and the loaves, "Even after he had served all the prisoners, the basket and the gourd were still full" (Giffords 1974:29). Seeing the miracle, the prisoners recognized the Child as an apparition of Christ himself.

In Mexico, the image of el Niño has become "an overwhelming favorite among the representations of Christ in this folk tradition" (Giffords 1974:29). Images of el Niño may be found in a variety of churches and sanctuaries throughout the country, but his principal place of worship is the small town of Plateros, near Fresnillo, Zacatecas.

Although the origins of el Niño at this location are somewhat obscure, we know that by 1566, a small settlement had grown up around the Mines of San Demetrio, later christened the Real de Minas de los Plateros (The Royal Mines of the Silverworkers). At some point during the eighteenth century, the mine's Spanish owner, the Marquis of San Miguel de Aguayo, commissioned a replica of Nuestra Señora de Atocha (with the Child in her arms), an image he had venerated in his homeland, to display in the sanctuary (Juárez Frías 1991).

During the colonial era, more homage appears to have been paid to the image of Nuestra Señora de Atocha than to the Child itself. During the 1820s, however, patterns of popular veneration shifted, and el Niño became separated from the image of the Virgin and given a special place in the sanctuary above the main altar (López de Lara 1992). Juárez Frías (1991) attributes this transformation to an unrecorded, but portentous, miracle that was attributed to el Niño in 1829. He also sees the shift as symbolic of the emancipation of the Mexican people from the mother country, because it occurred just after the conclusion of Mexico's Wars of Independence.

Dates engraved in the sanctuary's window casings indicate that the building was completed around 1790—before the supposed shift in allegiances—and decorative friezes depicting scenes from the life and passion of Christ suggest that the sanctuary was always intended to commemorate Christ rather than the Virgin (López de Lara 1992). Thus, the precise date for the emergence of the Child as a distinct object of veneration in Mexico remains somewhat unclear. All we can conclude is that the shift appears to have occurred at the end of the eighteenth or the beginning of the nineteenth century.

The image currently in use dates only from 1886, but according to Giffords (1974:29) it does not differ radically from earlier incarnations. Judging from its present appearance, el Niño was created from some kind of plaster, perhaps employing a variation of the Tarascan technique of titzingueni. In the sanctuary, the image sits upon a golden chair that rests on a golden pedestal. The Child's right hand holds a pilgrim's staff, on which a gourd is hung (representing water for the Christian captives), while the left hand holds a golden basket (symbolizing food for the prisoners). He wears a white robe streaked with gold and bound at the waist by a golden cord. On his blond hair rests a black hat adorned with a white plume, and his feet are clad in sandals (López de Lara 1992).

Although the foregoing image is frequently represented in votive art, equally common is another well-known image of the Holy Child of Atocha. Handed down from Catholic tradition, this representation is known as el Niño Azul (the Blue Child). Clad in a blue gown, brown cape, and a white lace collar, this Child is seated on a red upholstered chair, and the placement of the symbolic artifacts is reversed: the right hand now contains the basket while the left contains the pilgrim's staff and gourd. The left hand also holds a sprig of wheat, symbolizing the bread for the prisoners (and also possibly the Eucharist loaf). A cockleshell is fastened to the cape (indicating a pilgrim from Campostela, Spain), and the image is flanked to either side by a vase of flowers (Juárez Frías 1991; López de Lara 1992).

Documents deposited in the Archives of the Archdiocese of Zacatecas record that in 1882 Archbishop José María del Refugio Guerra y Alva visited the sanctuary, and upon seeing the great quantity of ex-votos fastened to its walls, was so impressed with the devotion of the people toward el Niño that he ordered the construction of a special chamber dedicated solely to the display of retablos (López de Lara 1991, 1992). On the Child's feast day, December 24, this Salón de Retablos is thronged with pilgrims from all over Mexico who come to pay homage to the revered image and leave their votive offerings.

▼

Images of the Virgin
La Virgen de Zapopan

Although images of Christ may command devoted followings in many communities, the Virgin Mary is even more widely venerated throughout Mexico, and we have included three of the western region's most important images in our study. The first is the Virgin of Zapopan, whose story begins in 1541, when Fray Antonio de Segovia arrived in the village of Zapopan ("place of the zapote tree," the zapote being a small fruit), located just outside the city of Guadalajara. He arrived carrying a breviary, a crucifix, and a small image of Nuestra Señora de la Concepción. According to legend, the image was half-formed when Fray Antonio arrived, but through a miracle it was made whole shortly after his arrival (Alvarez 1987).

From what is known of the image of the Virgin of Zapopan, its origin is more mundane than legend would have it. Like the images of Christ at Mineral de Cata and San Luis Potosí, it was sculpted from a mixture of corn paste and orchid juice using the titzingueni technique pioneered by the Tarascans, indicating an origin in Michoacán sometime around 1531 (Fray Antonio is said to have carried it with him for ten years before arriving in Zapopan). Juárez Frías (1991:81) attributes it directly to one of the workshops of Vasco de Quiroga.

Only the Virgin's hands are made from wood; the carved pieces are pressed together in prayer and attached to the image's chest (Alvarez 1987), a pose that follows the standard iconography for the Virgin of the Immaculate Conception in the fifteenth century (Giffords 1974:48–49). In 1935 the image was encased in a silver vessel over which a wardrobe of luxurious vestments is conspicuously displayed, leaving only the head and hands exposed.

The Virgin of Zapopan wears a light blue gown covered with a cape of the same color, but at times she may also be clad in a white. Both cape and gown are richly brocaded in gold and fringed with gilded tassels. The Virgin carries a golden scepter inlaid with pearls and rubies and holds a golden staff and the symbolic keys to the city of Guadalajara. Resting upon the image's flowing brown hair is a jewel-encrusted crown of golden arcs that rise from a broad band around the head to meet at the base of a golden cross (Alvarez 1987).

Marian iconography of the fifteenth century depicted the Virgin of the Immaculate Conception as Saint John's Woman of the Apocalypse: "Clothed by the sun, and the moon under her feet, and upon her head a crown of twelve stars" (Giffords 1974:48–49). The pedestal on which the Virgin sits alludes to this origin, for it contains a crescent moon facing upward with a row of stars underneath.

The first miracle attributed to the Virgin of Zapopan occurred upon her arrival in the community in 1541, when her presence pacified an Amerindian uprising on the hill of Mixtón, a feat for which she became known as la Pacificadora (the Pacifier [see Juárez Frías 1991]). In 1606, another miracle transpired when the image survived the collapse of the church without suffering even a scratch. Later the Virgin was reported to have miraculously restored sight to a blind man (Alvarez 1987).

In 1641 the priest Diego de Herrera, impressed with the powers of the Virgin, began collecting and publishing the miracles attributed to her. In 1653 Bishop Juan Ruiz Comenero decreed that the image was indeed miraculous and established December 18 as the Virgin of Zapopan's fiesta day. When a plague swept the city of Guadalajara in 1693, it ended only when Bishop Juan Sánchez de León Garabito ordered the image to be carried through the streets of the city. In 1721, the Virgin was brought to the deathbed of Bishop Manuel de Mimbela and restored him to life for four additional days. On September 15, 1821, the Virgin of Zapopan was once again paraded through the streets of Guadalajara to celebrate Mexico's Independence and to honor the proclamation of the image as the "Sovereign of Jalisco" by Bishop Juan Cruz Ruiz de Cabañas.

The original church of Zapopan collapsed in 1606, and a new edifice was built shortly thereafter. In 1690, however, Bishop Santiago de León Garabito initiated work on a larger and more impressive sanctuary, and 40 years later, in 1730, the image was installed on its present altar. Renovations were carried out on the structure in 1819, 1837, and 1867; and in 1889 the original bell towers were demolished and replaced with new ones, completed in 1892. In 1905 the altar was reconstructed in white marble and in 1940 the church was designated as a Basilica by Pope Pius XII (Alvarez 1987). Although the yearly number of votaries does not approach that observed at the Sanctuary of San Juan de los Lagos, it nonetheless remains a well-known image of votive supplication in western Mexico.

La Virgen de Talpa

Although obscure, the origins of the Virgin of Talpa also go back to the early colonial period. Like the Virgin of Zapopan, the image was created in the late sixteenth century by Amerindian artisans working under Bishop Vasco de Quiroga of Michoacán. The statue is small, only about 15 inches tall, and is made from corn pith using the Tarascan technique of titzingueni (Carrillo Dueñas 1986).

The principal difference between the Virgin of Talpa and Virgin of Zapopan is the former's underlying identity as la Virgen del Rosario (the Virgin of the Rosary), rather than the Virgin of the Immaculate Conception. The Virgin of the Rosary is the patroness of the Dominican Order and is typically depicted holding the Child Jesus in her left arm and a rosary in her right hand. In standard iconography she wears a blue cape over a red gown embroidered with blue trim (Juárez

Frías 1991:84). In Talpa, she sits on a silver pedestal with the moon inscribed at her feet and wears a gold crown encircled with precious stones. She is covered with a dress adorned with stars and triangle-shaped pearls (Carrillo Dueñas 1986).

The town of Talpa is located in the western Sierra Madre mountains in the state of Jalisco near the cities of Mascota and Ameca, both of which are now linked to the town by road. The settlement was founded in 1599 near the mine of Aranjuez, which was located atop a rich vein of silver that was later exhausted. The image was probably brought to town by Father Manuel de San Martín, the first priest to arrive in the region (Carrillo Dueñas 1986). Later the image of the Virgin was moved to "Los Reyes" mine, where it remained until a local Amerindian, Diego Felipe, once again brought it to Talpa.

Until 1644 the image occupied a secondary location in the church and had with time become rather worm-eaten and had lost much of its original beauty and luster. In that year the parish priest decided to remove the image from its alcove, and given its dilapidated state, he told a humble Amerindian woman, María Tenanchi, to clean it up. When she tried to fulfill her charge, however, she could not, because upon touching it she was dazzled by an intense light that emanated from inside the tiny figure (Carrillo Dueñas 1986).

Other women came running to investigate the source of the strange light, and the same thing happened when they tried to touch it. Their amazement only increased when they discovered that somehow the image had recovered its original luster and all signs of its deterioration had disappeared. The miracle was later confirmed by the townspeople and by civil and ecclesiastical authorities, who arrived from the neighboring town of Mascota to investigate. The miracle transformed the Virgin of the Rosary into the Patroness of the town, displacing the community's old patron saint, the Apostle Santiago.

Over the years, the fame of the little Virgin increased and the number of miracles attributed to her grew. In 1670, the Catholic Church launched an official investigation of the Virgin's miraculous origins and confirmed them in a document entitled, "Auténtica relación del milagro de la renovación de la milagrosa imagen de Nuestra Señora del Rosario de Talpa" (The True Account of the Miracle of the Renovation of the Miraculous Image of Our Lady of the Rosary of Talpa), a copy of which, dated 1832, has been preserved in the parish archives. In addition to narrating the story of the image's origins, the document offers testimony by witnesses to her miracles.

The main section of the present sanctuary was built in the second half of the eighteenth century, and the facade and towers were completed during the middle of the nineteenth century. A pontifical coronation was bestowed upon the Virgin on September 19, 1915, the 271st anniversary of her miraculous renovation. Although her fame has spread beyond Talpa over the years, the image's devotées remain concentrated in the area of western Jalisco and Nayarit, principally in the Sierra Madre mountains and along the coast.

Within this area, the Virgin of Talpa remains the most important image, and year after year thousands of pilgrims arrive to fulfill their vows, attend mass, and deposit their votives of thanks. Since the end of the seventeenth century, the fiesta of the Virgin of Talpa has been on February 2, a date that coincides with the dry season in Mexico, permitting pilgrims to undertake arduous journeys over difficult, and mostly unpaved, roads that wind through the surrounding hills and mountains.

The town has adapted to its status as a pilgrimage center and has evolved an economy that offers food, lodging, religious materials, and other services to the masses of pilgrims who come each year. Some devotees journey from as far away as the United States; for like other parts of western Mexico, Talpa has produced a host of international migrants. Not all return home to pay their respects, however; for such is the devotion to the image that a replica of the Virgin of Talpa has been installed in San Fernando, California, where migrants from the central valley and even Los Angeles come to pay their respects.

La Virgen de San Juan de los Lagos

Although each of the foregoing images has attracted significant veneration by some inhabitants of western Mexico, by far the most important icon in the region is the Virgin of San Juan de los Lagos (Olveda 1980; Alvarez 1987). The town of San Juan is located in a region of Jalisco known as los Altos (the highlands), aptly named for its high chaparral of windswept hills and dry pastures. Since early in the century, this area has been a center of migration to the United States (see Taylor 1933; Cornelius 1976). The town itself is situated in a shallow valley carved out of the surrounding hills by the San Juan River. The rolling hills and craggy ridges contain a number of small ponds and lakes that give the community its name: Saint John of the Lakes.

The legend of the Virgin of San Juan began in 1542, when a small image of the Virgin of the Immaculate Conception was brought into town by a Spanish priest, Father Miguel de Bologna (Alvarez 1987). Little is recorded of the image until 1623, when legend relates that the young daughter of two Amerindians, Pedro Andrés and Ana Lucía, fell gravely ill and seemed destined for an early grave; but in answer to the parents' fervent prayers the Virgin interceded and the girl was miraculously cured (Alvarez 1987). After the miracle, the image established its own Mexican identity, distinct from that of the Virgin of the Immaculate Conception, and since that time it has been known simply as the Virgin of San Juan (Alvarez 1987; Oblate Fathers 1991).

As news of the miracle spread, a growing number of Spanish settlers were drawn to the community, and Amerindian and mestizo pilgrims also began arriving in large numbers. Beginning in the early 1600s, a market fair developed around the anniversary of the image's installation on November 30. In 1630, some 2,000 persons were reported to have journeyed to San Juan for the festivities, and by 1792 the number of participants had reached 35,000.

Local authorities asked the King of Spain to recognize the market as a legal holiday and he granted the request in 1797, when the fair was decreed to begin on November 20 and run for 12 days thereafter. In 1840, attendance peaked at roughly 100,000 persons, but as industrialization and economic growth advanced during the nineteenth century, the crowds gradually declined and the market was finally abandoned shortly after the turn of the century (Olveda 1980). Currently the Virgin's anniversary is celebrated with a fiesta and pilgrims, but no longer a market or fair.

Like the image in Zapopan, the Virgin of San Juan was sculpted using a mixture of corn pith and orchid juice following the titzingueni technique, again suggesting Tarascan origins during the early sixteenth century. Standing about 20 inches tall, the Virgin is typically rendered in full view with her hands clasped in front of her breast (Alvarez 1987), consistent with fifteenth-century iconography for the Virgin of the Immaculate Conception (Giffords 1974:48–49).

Shortly after the Conquest, it became popular in Spain to affect greater realism in the presentation of the Virgin by giving images a lifelike face and hands, but mounting them on a mannequin-like body that could be clothed in sumptuous garments and tailored according to the fashions of the day (Giffords 1974:34). Existing statues were not discarded; they were simply "modernized" by enclosing them within pyramid-shaped frames that could be "dressed" lavishly.

Such a modernization was carried out on the Virgin of San Juan, probably during the late sixteenth century or early seventeenth century. Like the Virgin of Zapopan, she is enclosed in a frame that is covered with luxurious garments that leave only her head and hands exposed. The Virgin's light-skinned countenance arises out of a ruffled white collar to reveal long, light brown hair topped by a golden, jewel-encrusted tiara. The collar adorns a white gown accented with green-stemmed red roses. The gown is covered with a blue robe, embroidered with gold, pearls, and precious jewels, that is fastened at the neck and open in front to reveal the white gown underneath. (Alvarez 1987; Giffords 1991:46). The blue robe and white gown give the Virgin her characteristic colors, but she is also occasionally dressed in pure white.

In the sanctuary, the Virgin sits atop an ornate altar constructed in the sanctuary's principal apse. The altar, made of white marble decorated with gold trim, consists of a long platform roughly ten feet wide and five feet tall; on top sits a marble cupola flanked by sculpted angels and supported by eight six-foot-tall Ionic columns whose bases and capitals are made of silver burnished with gold. A multitude of candles placed in golden candelabras sit to either side of the Virgin's cupola, and at the center is a reliquary enclosed in a golden alcove. The whole arrangement is surrounded by the imposing columns of the sanctuary, which are also trimmed ornately in gold.

Underneath the cupola the Virgin rests on a golden pedestal. Relating to the image's original identity as the Virgin of the Immaculate Conception, the pedestal contains an upturned crescent moon engraved in gold and adorned with rubies and emeralds; under it are 12 stars made of precious stones. In santos paintings, the Virgin of San Juan is typically shown resting on this pedestal flanked by two candles (see the cover of Giffords 1991). In ex-votos, however, these elements are often omitted and replaced by a simple garland of clouds or a golden halo.

The first stone of the present church was laid on November 30, 1732, and construction continued for 58 years. The Virgin was installed on the main altar on November 30, 1769, but the bell towers, which rise 63 meters into the air, were not finished until 1790. Each tower consists of three tiers of sculpted neoclassical columns stacked on top of one another and capped by a golden cupola, on which one final tier of columns supports an ornate cross that can be seen throughout the valley.

Pilgrims are not permitted to leave votive offerings in the main sanctuary of the Basilica. A special chamber was added for this purpose in 1836 by order of Pope Gregory XVI and consecrated by the Archbishop of Guadalajara in November 1884 (Alvarez 1987). Located to the right of the main altar, the Chamber of the Virgin is filled with thousands of votive offerings, which arrive by the score each day. All available wall space is covered with paintings and objects left by grateful supplicants to thank the Virgin for miracles and favors they have received. Ex-votos layer the walls, spill out onto the floor, and climb toward the ceiling.

Yet even this chamber cannot contain all the retablos that pour into the chamber each year from the faithful. Two blocks away, the Virgin is represented at another pilgrimage site known as el Pocito (the little well) at the mouth of a natural spring. The site consists of a two-story, block-long, open-air balcony that has been constructed to house the Virgin's retablos. Its walls are also covered with ex-votos going back 80 years or more. In a recent effort to conserve and preserve the paintings, priests have placed the retablos of el Pocito under lock and key, grouped them by artist, and fastened them together so that they cover all available wall space from floor to ceiling.

La Virgen de San Juan: Holy Mother of Migrants

The yearly arrival of thousands of votaries in San Juan de los Lagos suggests the important role that retablos continue to play in the popular culture of western Mexico. In religious terms, these paintings provide a way of expressing devotion to a favored icon. In cultural terms, they represent one of the few means by which common people can give public expression to their anxieties, needs, fears, and sufferings. By objectifying their troubles in the form of a small painting on tin and setting it out for public display, ordinary people find some measure of release from life's vicissitudes.

Retablos are thus a catharsis, a personal testimony, a confession, an expression of gratitude or remorse that would otherwise be difficult to articulate publicly. Retablos give voice to the joys, celebrations, sufferings, illnesses, disgraces, enmities, losses, and tragedies of the human condition. As Diego Rivera put it simply, retablos are the "one true and present pictorial expression of the Mexican people" (Rivera 1979:55).

Troubles are not left behind, of course, when Mexicans move northward. Indeed, normal human problems multiply and entirely new difficulties arise. Not only do all the usual vexations continue; now they must be reconciled at a distance in a location far from home. Not only do people continue to get sick, have run-ins with the law, and struggle against forces beyond their control; now they must handle the same daunting situations in a strange language following a set of cultural rules they may only dimly understand.

Migrants, moreover, experience a set of special problems unique to their status as foreigners who are frequently undocumented. As surreptitious migrants, they undertake risky and dangerous border crossings; they regularly expose themselves to exploitation on the job and in daily life; they navigate a strange economy and an alien society; they have unpleasant encounters with powerful and arbitrary bureaucracies; and they live clandestinely outside the normal protection of legal authority.

It is not surprising, therefore, that holy images occupy a special place in the hearts of Mexican migrants to the United States. Through faith and devotion to familiar icons, people are able to make sense of the alienating and disjointed experiences of life in a foreign society. Holy images provide a cultural anchor for people adrift in a sea of strange experiences, exotic tongues, and odd customs. Icons such as the Virgin of San Juan provide a reassuring source of solace that enables migrants to construct an inner Mexico within the alien material culture of the United States.

Thus, when migrants experience moments of duress and anxiety in the course of their wanderings, they typically turn to a sacred image to assuage their apprehensions and calm their fears. As one woman who waded through sewage canals and hid from border police while crossing the frontier later recalled in a letter home, "If I am here it is because I believe in God and at those moments I asked the Virgin of Guadalupe, Juguila, and the Virgin of Solitude [to help me]" (Siems 1992:6–7). Devotion to a revered image symbolizes the expatriates' attachment to the language, culture, and people of Mexico; and leaving these symbols behind brings real psychological trauma and a tangible sense of loss.

One popular folk ballad transcribed by Taylor (1935:222–24) put this sentiment to music. The song adopts the viewpoint of a departing migrant who bids farewell to the various icons he passes on his way northward to work in the United States. Leaving his home in Guanajuato, the emigrant first faces south to ask the Virgin of Guadalupe for a safe return. As he travels to the north he pays homage successively to the principal images of his home state: la Madre de la Luz in Salvatierra, la Virgen de la Purísima Concepción in Celaya, el Señor del Hospital in Salamanca, la Madre de Loretito in Irapuato, and la Virgen de la Soledad in León. Traveling through Aguascalientes he enters Zacatecas and pauses at Plateros to say goodbye to el Niño de Atocha. Moving by train through Durango and Chihuahua, he finally arrives at Ciudad Juárez, on the Mexico-United States border, where he turns to offer a final goodbye to Guadalupe (see Fernández [1983], Fernández and Officer [1989], and Herrera-Sobek [1979] for other analyses of migrants' ballads).

One way of ameliorating the sense of cultural loss and psychological alienation that Mexicans feel while living and working in the United States is by bringing the venerated images northward. As one old woman in a small Texas town told us in an interview, "Seeing that this town was lost, and that my husband wanted to work here, well, I thought of having the Virgin [of San Juan] here so that my children could grow up well" (B. Villezcas, 1991).

Given the intense devotion of Mexicans to their images and the large and growing number of migrants living north of the border, Mexican communities in the United States have organized annual "tours" for several of the leading images. A replica of the Virgin of San Juan de los Lagos, for example, leaves Jalisco each year to visit churches in San Antonio, Los Angeles, Chicago, and other cities with large emigrant communities. At these locations, a parish in a predominantly Mexican neighborhood will inevitably have an altar or chapel dedicated to the Virgin (in Chicago, it is in St. Procopius Church in the Mexican neighborhood of Pilsen). The arrival of the Virgin is celebrated with special novenas and masses, and devotees pack the church and fill the altar with candles and a variety of votive objects (but not retablos).

In the late 1940s, Mexican immigrants living in the lower Rio Grande valley of Texas took their devotion to the Virgin of San Juan one step further. Rather than waiting each year for the arrival of the image from Jalisco, the parishioners of the small town of San Juan, Texas, prevailed on their priest, a Spanish Basque by the name of José María Aspiázu, to install a replica of the Virgin of San Juan in their own parish church. In 1949 he and two members of the congregation journeyed to Guadalajara to commission a leading sculptor to fashion an exact copy of the image. Three months later the work was ready, and they returned to Guadalajara to collect it (Aspiázu 1991; Oblate Fathers 1991; Pérez, 1991; B. Villezcas 1991).

The image of the Virgin of San Juan was installed in a special nook of the parish church on December 5, 1949. Impressed with the "explosion of faith" that followed, Father Aspiázu decided to construct a new chapel dedicated solely to the Virgin of San Juan. He and a young parishioner,

Benito Villezcas, taped a radio program that announced this intention and solicited contributions from Mexicans in the area. With the first transmission, from a Spanish-language station in Edinburg, Texas, they received 18 letters with donations of money (Aspiázu 1991). As the weekly quarter-hour programs continued, the volume of mail grew and the broadcast was aired by other stations throughout Texas, including stations in Corpus Christi, Lubbock, Houston, San Antonio, and Laredo. Eventually nine stations carried the broadcast to places as distant as California and Wisconsin (Aspiázu 1991; J. Villezcas 1991).

Within a year, the contributions were coming in so fast that 13 volunteers were kept busy for three hours every night sorting the letters and counting the donations that arrived from all over the United States. Money came not only from nearby cities such as Dallas, El Paso, Houston, and San Antonio, but also from the West Coast and the Midwest (J. Villezcas 1991).

With these donations, and with materials and labor donated by parishioners, work on the new church began in 1952. The sanctuary was inaugurated by the Bishop of Corpus Christi on Sunday, April 25, 1954, in the presence of 60,000 Mexican migrants who had come from all over the United States to witness the occurrence (Aspiázu 1991; Oblate Fathers 1991). The event was celebrated with special masses, novenas, parades, and other festivities.

After the inauguration, radio programs continued to spread the virtues of la Virgen de San Juan del Valle, as the image came to be known, and donations and pilgrims flooded in. With the additional contributions, a school, a home for the aged, and eventually a 90-room hotel were added to the complex (Aspiázu 1991; Sánchez 1991).

In 1970, the astounding success of the Catholic shrine infuriated a local fundamentalist preacher who was a pilot. In a mad attempt to extirpate the Virgin and cut short her success, he undertook a suicide mission and crashed his plane directly into the sanctuary. Although 92 priests were celebrating a special mass at the time, miraculously no one was killed and the Virgin survived the ensuing inferno unscathed (Aspiázu 1991; Reyna 1991).

Ironically, by destroying the old church, the preacher unintentionally did the parishioners of San Juan, Texas, a favor, because with the money they received from the insurance settlement they replaced the old 800-person chapel with a new sanctuary large enough to hold 4,000 people, with space for another 1,000 in temporary seating (Aspiázu 1991). Thanks to his misplaced efforts, the fame of the Virgin was heightened further.

The Virgin of San Juan del Valle now provides solace and solidarity to a vast network of migrants in the United States. The shrine receives around 10,000 weekly visitors during peak periods (estimated by Reyna [1991] from the number of communion wafers consumed) and now has 90 employees divided between the sanctuary, a hotel, a cafeteria, a maintenance department, a mail room, an accounting unit, and a retail store.

The shrine also maintains its own publishing enterprise, which manages a mailing list of some 120,000 names. Every month the shrine sends out 40,000 letters to faithful devotées of the Virgin scattered throughout the United States, and about 100,000 letters arrive each month from Mexican migrants in the United States. Between 60 percent and 70 percent of these express thanks to the Virgin for one of three things: crossing the Rio Grande safely, obtaining legal residence papers, or getting a job in the United States (Salazar 1991). Almost all the pilgrims who visit the shrine are Mexican immigrants traveling from locations in the United States; very few make the journey from Mexico.

Processions with floats and mariachis are regularly held every August 15 and December 8, and novenas are periodically scheduled throughout the year. Although the Virgin of San Juan del Valle is an important source of moral support for Mexicans in the United States, the image does not support a tradition of votive painting. Father Aspiázu (1991) does recall seeing some votive art in the shrine's early days, and Gamio (1930:122) mentions retablos prepared by migrants in San Antonio during the 1920s; but the custom of leaving painted ex-votos is apparently not presently observed at U.S. sanctuaries.

When migrants prepare a retablo of thanks for some miracle received, they make a journey back to the land of their birth, and each year thousands of Mexican migrants do precisely this, trekking back to Fresnillo, San Felipe, Mineral de Cata, Tepatitlán, Plateros, Zapopan, Talpa, or San Juan de los Lagos. It is to the outcome of these pilgrimages, the beautiful and compelling "masterpieces on tin" (from Giffords 1974) that we now turn.

5
▼▼▼

THE CONTENT OF
MIGRANTS' RETABLOS

ur interest in the retablos of Mexican migrants to the United States began in September of 1988, when we traveled to the church of San Juan de los Lagos to visit the Chamber of the Virgin and see her famous votive paintings. As we admired the colorful pictures and dramatic texts, we noted several that dealt with experiences in the United States. As students of Mexico-United States migration, our interest was piqued and we began to look for more of these paintings. Within an hour, we had located a dozen votives left by U.S. migrants.

As we reflected on these works, it occurred to us that they might shed new light on a well-worn topic. Unlike other sources of information on transnational migration, retablos capture events as they were experienced by the migrants themselves. The pictures and texts provide a rich source of historical and sociological data on a subject that has been notoriously resistant to study. Because they depict salient events at the moment of their occurrence, moreover, they provide an immediate record of migrants' most pressing concerns. By scrutinizing these paintings, we can catch a glimpse of moments in the U.S. migration experience and sense how they were felt and understood by the people who experienced them.

During the period from September 1988 through December 1993, we deliberately sought out religious shrines in western Mexico known to support a votive tradition, and we scoured galleries and antique dealers looking for retablos that somehow touched upon the subject of U.S. migration. In religious sanctuaries we took photographs and transcribed texts whenever we came upon a retablo that dealt in any way with migration to the United States, and in private galleries we purchased any such retablo that we encountered.

Over the course of the investigation, we located some 124 retablos painted or commissioned by U.S. migrants or their relatives. The scenes and texts contained in these votive works constitute the basic data for our study. In each case, we have a photograph of the painting and a transcription of the text, and in 61 cases we own the reproduced retablo. We include in our analysis any votive painting that we judged to have been left by a current or former migrant to the United States, or by a member of his or her family. Clues used to establish the identity of the donor include the place where the event in question occurred, the place of residence of the supplicant, the subject matter of the painting, the language used in the text, and in some cases the names of the actors involved.

All of the retablos were executed on a durable medium, in most cases tin. Of the 124 retablos we examined, 114 (92 percent) were painted on metal, five were on masonite, and three were on wood. Only two are executed on paper, and they are both enclosed in a glass frame and mounted on a durable backing. We chose to focus on durable media in order to control for the selective way that votive paintings survive. Although we can observe contemporary votive offerings on all sorts of perishable media, we can only observe past works that have been painted on something that is likely to have survived. Thus, any survey reconstructed from retablos of the past is likely to be more highly selective than one pieced together from votive materials encountered in the present. In order to hold constant the degree of selection over time, we focus our attention primarily on retablos that have been painted on the most durable of materials: tin.

Because ex-votos at times address multiple icons, the 124 works we examine contain 129 separate holy images, the distribution of which is shown in Table 5.1. By far the most popular image is the Virgin of San Juan de los Lagos, which constitutes roughly half of the icons referenced. As we have already noted, no other image approaches the Virgin of San Juan in attracting the devotion of migrants to the United States. The next closest figure is that of el Niño de Atocha,

Table 5.1. Distribution of Retablos Examined in
Study by Image of Supplication

Sacred Image	Number	Percentage
Images of the Virgin Mary		
Virgen de San Juan	64	49.6
Virgen de Talpa	5	3.9
Virgen de Zapopan	4	3.1
Virgen de Guadalupe	4	3.1
Virgen de los Remedios	1	0.8
Images of Christ		
El Niño de Atocha	10	7.7
Señor de la Conquista	9	7.0
Señor de la Villaseca	8	6.2
Senor de la Misericordia	5	3.9
Señor del Saucito	5	3.9
Images of Saints		
San Miguel	7	5.4
San Martín de Porres	4	3.1
San Martín de Terreros	1	0.8
San Francisco de Asis	1	0.8
San Judas Tadeo	1	0.8
Total Images Mentioned	129	100.0%

with about 8 percent of the images, followed by el Señor de la Conquista (7 percent) and el Señor de Villaseca (6 percent).

Closely related to the image of el Señor de la Conquista is that of San Miguel (forming about 5 percent of the sample). This minor icon is located in a small chapel in the sanctuary of San Felipe Torres Mochas, the same pilgrimage site for el Señor de la Conquista. La Virgen of Talpa, el Señor de la Misericordia, and el Señor del Saucito each add another 4 percent of the images to the sample, and the Virgins of Zapopan and Guadalupe another 3 percent.

Although U.S. migrants share many of the same problems as others who bring votives before a sacred image, the experience of transnational migration yields a set of singular issues that distinguish them from other supplicants. A typology of retablos developed for general use, such as that of Creux (1979), is therefore of limited utility in attempting to comprehend and classify the range of problems experienced by U.S. migrants.

Although, like other votaries, international migrants may face illness, catastrophe, war, fire, falling, work, and animal problems (Creux's categories), the meaning of these problems is very different in a foreign context; and migrants face other unique difficulties that set them distinctly apart. These problems include the pain of separation from loved ones; the hazards of moving north; the risks of crossing the border; the fear of falling sick in a strange land; the threat of arrest and deportation; and the thorny issue of documentation.

In view of these distinctive concerns, we developed our own categorization of retablos that builds on the earlier efforts of Creux and others, but which takes into account the unusual situation of U.S. migrants. The typology contains six major headings and 16 detailed subcategories. The major headings follow the course of a migrant's journey to and from the United States. They include "Making the Trip," "Finding One's Way," "Legal Problems," "Medical Problems," "Getting By in the United States," and "Homecoming." Under these broad rubrics, we define 16 subcategories that address particular topics.

In order to carry out a detailed content analysis of retablos, we classified each ex-voto into one and only one of the 16 subcategories. In cases where more than one subcategory could have applied, we classified the retablo according to the subject that, in our judgment, was dominant. The results of this operation are shown in Table 5.2.

The first general heading is "Making the Trip," and it considers three salient issues involved in moving from Mexico to the United States. Difficulties encountered while traveling north fall into the first subcategory and those faced while crossing the border make up the second. The third subcategory focuses on the special problems that women face in going north. As Table 5.2 indicates, nearly 15 percent of the retablos in our sample deal in some way with one of these themes.

Roughly 2 percent of the pictures fall into the subcategory "Heading North." A good example under this rubric is the retablo left by a woman from León, Guanajuato, who was traveling north to the United States in October 1946 when the roadway suddenly washed out and several of her companions were swept away. Fearing the worst, she called upon the Virgin of San Juan and

Table 5.2. Distribution of Retablos Examined in
Study by Subject Matter

Subject	Number	Percentage
Making the Trip	18	14.5%
Heading North	3	2.4
Crossing the Border	11	8.9
Women's Issues	4	3.2
Finding One's Way	5	4.0%
Getting a Job	2	1.6
Getting Lost	3	2.4
Legal Problems	18	14.6%
Arranging Documents	8	6.5
Run-ins with the Law	10	8.1
Medical Problems	30	24.2%
Getting Sick	22	17.7
Having an Operation	8	6.5
Getting By in the U.S.	27	21.8%
War	7	5.7
Work Accidents	5	4.0
Traffic Accidents	12	9.7
Crime	1	0.8
Getting Ahead	2	1.6
Homecoming	22	17.7%
Grateful Migrants	7	5.6
Thankful Relatives	15	12.1
Unnamed Miracles	4	3.2%
Total Retablos Examined	124	100.0%

entrusted them to her protection; later they miraculously turned up unharmed, a piece of good fortune that she credited to the divine powers of the Virgin.

Another 3 percent of the compiled retablos come under the heading of "Women's Issues." One such painting, dated November 19, 1989, was left by María del Carmen Parra, who gives "thanks to the Holiest Virgin of San Juan de los Lagos for having granted that [my] daughter could marry in the United States." For many women, marriage to a migrant, a Chicano, or an Anglo American (from the retablo it is not clear who the husband is) provides a path of potential mobility to a better life, one free from the strictures of poverty and patriarchy in Mexico, and one to which mothers frequently aspire on behalf of their daughters (see Reichert 1982; Goldring 1992; Hondagneu-Sotelo 1992). In any event, the mother in this case felt sufficient gratitude to commemorate the marriage with a retablo.

By far the most frequently mentioned subject under the general heading of making the trip is "Crossing the Border," a subject that occupies 9 percent of the retablos in the sample. As this relatively high frequency indicates, the risks of border crossing loom large in the minds of Mexican migrants who lack legal documents and must enter the United States surreptitiously. In addition to the risk of arrest and deportation (according to the latest estimates, the odds of getting caught are about 33 percent on any attempt [see Espenshade 1990; Kossoudji 1992; and Donato et al. 1992]), undocumented migrants also face the hazards of fraud, injury, robbery, thirst, hunger, and drowning. Those who make it though the gauntlet of border-crossing hazards naturally feel indebted to a holy image for watching over them and often for delivering them from acute danger.

Angelina García Solís, for example, left a votive addressed to el Señor del Saucito "for the miracle that He granted me in the year 1949. Finding myself drowning in the waters of the Rio Grande in el Norte in the company of other friends, in the most desperate moment I invoked his help after I had given up hope. I give him a thousand and one thanks, and also to God, that through His mediation He did me such an immense favor." Another anonymous votary thanked the Virgin of Talpa for saving "me from death on September 20, 1948. Upon wishing to cross the Rio Grande, two friends were killed but I was able to save myself."

After a migrant has entered the United States, new difficulties arise and these are the subject of the second heading, "Finding One's Way," which comprises 4 percent of the retablos in our sample. Getting lost in a strange setting is a problem treated in about 2 percent of the retablos. Often this misfortune befalls migrants from small towns who arrive in large U.S. cities (a good example is presented in the next chapter) but it also occurs in the countryside, often in arid parts of California, Texas, or Arizona, where migrants travel for work. Ponciano Guzmán did not give details on his retablo of September 4, 1951, he just gave "thanks, to the Virgin of Zapopan for having gotten us out of this desert without harm."

A major part of finding one's way is getting a job, for without work migrants cannot repay the expenses of the trip, support themselves, or send money back home to family members in Mexico (Massey et al. 1987). About 2 percent of the retablos treat this theme. One of them was left by J. Melquides Murillo of Puerto de Loja, Guanajuato, who in 1961 gave "thanks to Holiest Mary of San Juan de los Lagos, because I prayed to her that I might go and come across the border and that I might be hired."

The third major heading is "Legal Problems," the subject of roughly 15 percent of the retablos in our sample. First and foremost in this category is the problem of documentation, because without a legal residence card or some other form of legal documentation, a person's tenure in the United States is insecure and can end at a moment's notice. As a result, undocumented migrants are vulnerable to exploitation and are confined to an underground economy of unstable, poorly paid jobs.

Nearly 7 percent of the retablos we sampled concerned the issue of documentation. One of them was left by Luz Bravo Magaña, who on November 8, 1945, simply offered "thanks to the Virgin of San Juan de los Lagos for the miracle of having obtained without difficulty my passport from the American consulate." (Anyone who has ever waited in line to get a visa at a U.S. embassy can appreciate how "miraculous" this event seemed.) In 1989, another man left a retablo giving thanks to the Virgin of San Juan "for having acted on the petitions that I made to you for my brother to get his visa."

A second subcategory, comprising another 8 percent of the sample, focuses on encounters with law enforcement officials, the most feared of whom are immigration officers. Migrants occasionally run afoul of other authorities, however, and at times end up in jail. For such people, the usual problems of loneliness and fear are magnified by the fact that incarceration isolates them in a strange culture and prevents them from seeing loved ones who remain in Mexico.

Within this subcategory is the offering of Juan Jaime Delgado who addressed his retablo to the "Lord of Villaseca that is venerated in the Sanctuary of Mineral de Cata. I give infinite thanks for helping me get out of jail in the United States and for arriving safely in the city of Guanajuato in the year 1986." In his retablo, José Gutiérrez likewise gave "thanks to the Lord Saint Michael for having saved me from a sentence of 20 years in a prison in Chicago, U.S.A., releasing me after only 8 months."

A fourth general heading is "Medical Problems," the largest content category in our sample. Getting sick is especially terrifying when one has no friends or family nearby, when one does not speak the language, and when one lacks money or insurance to pay doctor bills. About 18 percent of the retablos we sampled mentioned sickness in the United States. The gratitude that María de Jesús Torres felt after her daughter got well was such that she traveled all the way to Jalisco from her home in National City, California, to "offer infinite thanks to Our Lady of San Juan for having given health to my daughter, Teresa Torres, who suffered from asthma and epileptic attacks for several years."

Having to undergo an operation is also threatening when one cannot communicate effectively with the medical staff, or when one does not fully understand the medical system or its technology. About 7 percent of the retablos in our collection explicitly give thanks to an image for having survived a surgical procedure performed in the United States. On January 3, 1962, in Santa Fe, New Mexico, for example, Concepción González Anderson underwent a surgical procedure during which "they did an examination to see if I had cancer. Thanks to the Holiest Virgin of San Juan, I was spared from this sickness for which I give infinite thanks for the miracle she gave me."

While living and working in the United States, Mexicans face a variety of additional issues related to well-being grouped under the fifth general heading, "Getting By in the United States," which comprises 22 percent of the retablos we assembled. Unlike Mexico, the United States is a global power with many foreign commitments; and if a person enlists in its armed forces, there exists the very real risk of having to go to war in a far-off place. Legal immigrants, as well as children of Mexicans born in the United States, are subject to the U.S. military draft (including the children of undocumented parents), and Mexican immigrants have fought in all major wars of the twentieth century, most recently in the Persian Gulf.

Among the 124 retablos we assembled, a total of 6 percent thanked an image for a safe return from war. The oldest such retablo we found was prepared by the uncle of Angel Turburán and deposited in the Sanctuary of el Señor de Villaseca on July 19, 1917. Referring to his nephew's service in World War One, the text states that "having been mortally wounded in the war, his uncle

Roberto Rodríguez, from . . . New Mexico, commended him to the Holiest Lord of Villaseca that he should not die. . . . Having cured him from his sickness he makes public this miracle."

Aside from the extreme case of warfare, Mexican migrants face other risks while abroad. One is accidents at work. Migrants tend to be employed in agriculture, construction, the garment industry, and small-scale manufacturing, hazardous sectors where employers are under intense competitive pressure. In order to keep expenses low, companies invest little in safety devices or new equipment, thereby increasing the risk of work-related accidents. Some 4 percent of the retablos in our sample mention an accident at work. One such retablo was left by Manuel Reyes, who found himself picking cotton near Brawley, California, during fall 1954 when he got his hand caught in some machinery. At this moment, he invoked the image of San Miguel, who intervened to free him, "losing a finger but saving my life, and in proof of gratitude I dedicate the present retablo."

Another 10 percent of the retablos in the sample revolve around traffic accidents, a danger especially prevalent among migrants traveling to large urban areas in the United States. In 1954, one grateful migrant gave "thanks to the Virgin of San Juan de los Lagos for having saved me from an automobile accident that occurred in San Francisco, California, in which four persons were left dead and four injured."

For Mexican migrants living in large U.S. cities, such as Los Angeles, crime constitutes another hazard of life in the United States, and one retablo in our collection (presented in the next chapter) deals with this issue. However, getting by in the United States is not simply a matter of surviving negative experiences such as crime and car accidents. Ubiquitous among the votive objects left in Mexican sanctuaries are tokens of some foreign success: a driver's license, a report card, a high school diploma, a college degree.

Although it is less common to find retablos commemorating these events, we did encounter two votive paintings that gave thanks for a personal achievement in the United States. One offered thanks to the Virgin of Zapopan for "having been able to obtain a nursing certificate in the U.S.A." Another, from a migrant in Los Angeles, thanked the same Virgin for "a miracle obtained in the artistic world some years ago."

The last phase of the migrant journey, "Homecoming," involves the return of migrants to the warmth of their families and to the familiar soil of their birth. Given the many hazards and difficulties faced in the course of a U.S. trip, migrants and their families are often overcome with gratitude when a long separation finally comes to an end. The strength of this emotion is such that a votive of thanks is commissioned and left at a local shrine. Roughly 18 percent of the retablos in our sample fell under the general heading "Homecoming," with 12 percent expressing the gratitude of family members and 6 percent offering thanks from the migrants themselves.

Typical of the grateful migrants was Tereso López, of Rancho de la Palma, near Silao, Guanajuato, who contributed a retablo on the occasion of his return to Mexico from the United States. In this votive painting he "gives thanks to the Holiest Virgin of San Juan. Finding himself in the United States and commending himself to the Virgin, he asked that upon arriving on his soil he would go to visit her."

A systematic analysis of the content of migrants' retablos provides a glimpse into the special problems and difficulties they face. If we simply list those subcategories with a relative frequency of 5 percent or more, we see that crossing the border, arranging documents, and avoiding encounters with legal authorities are principal preoccupations of U.S. migrants and that getting sick, having an operation, getting drafted, and experiencing traffic accidents are major risks of life in the United States. When they manage to overcome these problems and return home safely, migrants and their family members are filled with gratitude.

Additional insight can be gained by classifying the subject matter of migrants' retablos according to the period in which the trip took place (see the top panel of Table 5.3). This analysis employs five temporal categories: the first extends from 1900 to 1939 and represents the early years of Mexico-United States migration; the second runs from 1940 to 1964 and corresponds to the Bracero era, when the U.S. government sponsored a temporary labor program that brought some 4.5 million Mexicans into the United States to work (see Craig 1971; Samora 1971); the third period extends from 1965 to 1979, an era when Mexico-United States migration was growing rapidly; and the modern period ranges from 1980 to the present. A residual fifth category contains retablos whose date could not be firmly established.

The greatest number of retablos (27 percent) comes from the Bracero era (see the totals at the bottom of the table), followed in frequency by the modern era and the growth years (at about 19 percent each); the period with the fewest examples is the early years (around 9 percent). Roughly

26 percent of the retablos could not be dated with certainty. Given the limited number of retablos in our sample, we examine temporal shifts only in the main content categories.

Issues surrounding homecoming appear to be significant in all periods, with the exception of the Bracero era, when medical problems clearly dominate. The problem of getting by in the United States is notably salient in the early and growth years of U.S. migration. Although this category is also prevalent to some extent during the Bracero era, it is relatively underrepresented during the modern period. As transnational movement has become routine and institutionalized, issues

Table 5.3. Distribution of Retablos Examined in Study by Subject Matter, Gender of Supplicant, and Period of U.S. Migration

| | Period of Migration | | | | |
	Early Years 1900–39	Bracero Era 1940–64	Growth Years 1965–79	Modern Era 1980–93	Undated
Subject Matter					
Making Trip	18.2%	20.6%	4.4%	16.7%	12.5%
Finding Way	9.1	8.8	4.4	0.0	0.0
Legal Problems	9.1	5.9	13.0	29.1	15.8
Medical Problems	0.0	41.2	17.4	16.7	24.9
Getting By in U.S.	36.3	17.6	39.1	8.3	18.8
Homecoming	27.3	5.9	21.7	16.7	24.9
Unnamed	0.0	0.0	0.0	12.5	3.0
Gender of Supplicant					
Male	50.0%	48.5%	47.8%	66.7%	52.0%
Female	50.0	51.5	52.2	33.3	48.0
U.S. Destination					
Border Area	9.1%	20.6%	4.4%	12.5%	6.3%
California	0.0	26.5	26.1	16.7	15.6
Texas	18.2	14.7	21.7	12.5	9.4
Other	45.4	17.6	4.4	16.7	15.6
Unknown	27.3	20.6	43.4	41.6	53.1
Total Retablos	11	34	23	24	32
Percentage in Period	8.9%	27.4%	18.5%	19.4%	25.8%

relating to "Getting By" have receded into the background, because, unlike their predecessors, migrants arriving after 1980 can count on a host of friends, relatives, and compatriots, as well as a range of formal and informal contacts, to facilitate their entry and employment within the United States (Massey et al. 1994).

Perhaps the most striking trend over time is the increasing salience of legal problems, in particular those related to documentation. From the early to the modern era, the percentage of retablos dealing with legal problems increases from 9 percent to 29 percent; and after 1980, issues related to the acquisition of legal documents dominate all others. This trend reflects the fact that, since the late 1970s, U.S. law has become increasingly restrictive with respect to Mexican immigration.

In 1976, Mexico was placed under a quota of 20,000 immigrants for the first time, and in 1978 it was forced into a worldwide ceiling of 290,000 immigrants, which was subsequently reduced to 270,000 in 1980 (see Jasso and Rosenzweig 1990:28–29). These changes have made fewer immigrant visas available to Mexican nationals, causing those who do manage to acquire papers to be very grateful when they get them.

Retablos also provide important clues about the geographic origins and destinations of U.S. migrants, as well as their sex composition. It is common for suppliants to end a votive text with their name, community, and state of origin, information that can be used to discern the gender and geographic origins of migrants to the United States. Votive texts also commonly relate where the miraculous event occurred, and this information can be used to discern U.S. destination sites.

Reading and recovering pertinent information can sometimes be difficult, however. At times retablos are unsigned, or the gender of the name is ambiguous, making it impossible to determine the sex of the votary. In addition, U.S. place-names are typically rendered in phonetic Spanish equivalents, leading to many curious misspellings and confusing renditions of English words. Moreover, after weeks, months, or even years in a sanctuary, retablos invariably acquire a thick layer of dust, soot, wax, and grime that makes reading difficult. Often the paintings are inaccessible, hung 20 feet up a church wall or fastened beneath several other votive works. In some cases, priests have stacked dozens of retablos in piles on the floor in preparation for their removal.

Under these conditions, coming upon a migrant's retablo yields an emotional experience similar to that felt by the historian who finally stumbles upon a long-sought incunabulum or the archaeologist who at last discovers a missing artifact in a dark and dusty tomb. After the spark of recognition that a retablo once belonged to a U.S. migrant, the slow process of reading and discovery inevitably begins.

Table 5.4 shows the distribution of retablos in our sample broken down by gender, Mexican origin, and U.S. destination. In most cases, the gender of the supplicant could be established from the picture or the text. In general, men and women are about equally represented among votaries. Among the migrants who left paintings at the shrines we considered, 46 percent were men, 42 percent were women, and 12 percent were of unknown gender. Among those whose gender could be established from information included on the retablo, 53 percent were men and 47 percent were women.

A large number of the votive texts and paintings contained no information about geographic origins or destinations. Some 58 percent of the works provided no state or community of origin in Mexico, and 38 percent gave no geographic data about the destination in the United States. Frequently a U.S. destination was indicated only by the initials E.U. (Estados Unidos) or U.S.A., or by vague references to el norte.

The frequency of unknown places in Mexico probably reflects an assumption by votaries that unless the state of origin is named, it is implicitly understood to be that where the image is located. Because roughly 60 percent of the retablos in our sample are dedicated to images in Jalisco, a large share of the "unknown" retablos probably originate in that state, one that is notably underrepresented in the frequency distribution (only 2 percent of the retablos in the sample refer explicitly to Jalisco), especially given this state's prominence as a migrant-sending region.

Even allowing for the underrepresentation of retablos from Jalisco, however, the number of votive paintings from the state of Guanajuato is remarkable, testifying to its importance as a cradle for this popular artistic tradition. Nearly 30 percent of all the retablos in our collection, and nearly 70 percent of those whose origins are known, were prepared or commissioned by someone from Guanajuato, despite the fact that around 80 percent of the offerings were made to shrines in Jalisco, San Luis Potosí, or Zacatecas (see Table 5.1). A large number of supplicants must therefore have left Guanajuato to pay their respects to an image in another state, despite the fact that Guanajuato itself has several shrines with well-established votive traditions.

One state notable for its scarcity in Table 5.4 is Michoacán. Despite being situated in the

Table 5.4. Geographic Distribution of Mexican Origin and U.S. Destination Mentioned in Retablos Under Study

Gender or Place	Number	Percentage	Gender or Place	Number	Percentage
Gender of Supplicant			California	24	19.4
Male	57	46.0%	Los Angeles	10	8.1
Female	52	41.9	Other	14	11.3
Unknown	15	12.1	Texas	18	14.5
Mexican Origin			Other	21	16.9
Guanajuato	36	29.0%	Arizona	2	1.6
San Luis Potosí	6	4.8	Colorado (Denver)	3	2.4
Other	10	8.1	Florida	1	0.8
Aguascalientes	1	0.8	Idaho	1	0.8
Baja California	1	0.8	Illinois (Chicago)	6	4.8
Durango	1	0.8	Kansas	1	0.8
Jalisco	2	1.6	Michigan	1	0.8
Michoacán	2	1.6	Nebraska	1	0.8
Tamaulipas	1	0.8	New Mexico	3	2.4
Zacatecas	2	1.6	Ohio	1	0.8
Unknown	72	58.1	Wisconsin	1	0.8
U.S. Destination			Unknown	47	37.9
Border Region	14	11.3%	Total	124	100.0

heart of the west-central region, and although it traditionally has been one of the most important migrant-sending states in Mexico, only two retablos in the sample give Michoacán as a place of origin. This relative absence probably reflects, at least in part, the Amerindian heritage of the state, the homeland of the Tarascans. As discussed in chapter one, votive painting took hold most strongly in mestizo areas that were not directly evangelized by colonial priests. The only hint of a votive tradition in Michoacán is that surrounding Nuestra Señora de la Salud, in Pátzcuaro, another sixteenth-century image made from corn pith and orchid juice (Giffords 1974). Although this icon supported an active tradition of retablo painting before 1900 (see Montenegro 1950), it has now died out.

Aside from Guanajuato, the only other Mexican state mentioned with any frequency is San Luis Potosí (about 5 percent of the retablos in our collection), the home of el Señor del Saucito. Other states that receive mention are Aguascalientes and Zacatecas, in the western region, and the northern states of Baja California, Durango, and Tamaulipas. The community names listed on the retablos typically refer to tiny rural hamlets, often with poetic names such as Coesillo, Rancho de la Palma, or Rancho el Saucillo, suggesting the rural, campesino origin of many migrants to the United States.

The distribution of U.S. destinations mentioned in the retablos is shown in the bottom panel of Table 5.4 and serves to illustrate the uneven regional concentration of Mexican migrants to the United States (Bartel 1989; Jasso and Rosenzweig 1990). California and Texas together account for about 35 percent of the retablos in the sample, and 57 percent of those with known destinations. The most important single destination is Los Angeles (8 percent of the retablos in the sample), followed by Chicago (5 percent) and Denver (2 percent). Some 12 percent of the texts make a vague reference to some location along the border; and the remaining destinations are scattered throughout the Midwestern states of Illinois, Kansas, Nebraska, Ohio, Wisconsin, or among the Southwestern states of Arizona, Colorado, and New Mexico. One person mentioned a place-name in Florida.

We can shed additional light on U.S. destinations when we examine them according to period (see the bottom panel of Table 5.3). During the earliest period, migrant destinations were diverse and scattered, and California had not yet emerged as a significant area of attraction. A diversity of destinations is typical of migration flows during their early stages of evolution, before social networks and strong connections to employers arise to channel people to specific sites (see Jones 1981; Massey et al. 1994).

The shift to California occurred during the Bracero era, when the U.S. Department of Labor recruited large numbers of Mexicans for specialized work in that state's expanding agricultural economy. The dominance of California continued through the growth era as the relative importance of other states declined. Although destinations appear to have become more diverse again during the modern era, interpretation is clouded somewhat by the rather large number of retablos in the unknown category.

The middle panel of Table 5.3 shows trends in the gender composition of migrants across periods. In general, gender ratios are relatively even as one moves from the early years through the growth years of migration. It is only in the modern period, after 1980, that the gender composition becomes unbalanced, with a pronounced upward shift in the prevalence of men. The parallel increase in the frequency of legal problems suggests this shift may stem from the Immigration Reform and Control Act (IRCA) of 1986, which authorized a legalization program for undocumented agricultural workers, a group that is predominantly male. By requiring migrants to prove that they had worked in U.S. agriculture during 1985 or 1986, the program put a premium on documentation and thereby produced a bounty of retablos afterwards, in 1989 and 1990, from grateful men who had managed to qualify for legal status.

One last way of shedding light on the nature of Mexico-United States migration is to cross-tabulate gender and destination by content category (see Table 5.5). In general, men and women appear to be equally concerned with the problems of making the trip and getting by in the United States. Within these categories, the sex composition of votaries is about even. Among retablos dealing with legal and medical problems, however, female votaries are somewhat more prevalent, constituting about 60 percent of the votives mentioning these themes. Except for the most recent period that included IRCA, therefore, women appear to face legal issues in migration more frequently than men.

Two categories were dominated by males, however. All of the votive paintings that dealt with finding one's way in the United States were prepared by males, and 58 percent of those who expressed gratitude for homecoming were likewise men. When the latter category is broken into votives left by migrants and those left by family members, however, a pronounced gender disparity arises. All of the homecoming retablos left by migrants were commissioned or executed by men, but 62 percent of those offered by family members were left by women. To a considerable extent, it seems, men migrate while women remain behind and wait.

When destinations are classified by content categories we find, not surprisingly, that retablos concerned with making the trip are dominated by references to the border region (67 percent of all cases). In contrast, those focusing on legal problems refer to Texas or other states; and retablos dealing with life abroad generally mention Texas or California. Among votive works covering medical problems, for example, 37 percent were left by migrants from California and 27 percent

Table 5.5. Distribution of Retablos Examined in Study by Subject, Gender of Supplicant, and U.S. Destination

	Subject of Retablo					
	Making Trip	Finding Way	Legal Problems	Medical Problems	Getting By	Homecoming
Gender of Supplicant						
Male	50.0%	100.0%	40.0%	42.3%	45.8%	57.9%
Female	50.0	0.0	60.0	57.7	54.2	42.1
U.S. Destination						
Border	66.7%	20.0%	0.0%	0.0%	0.0%	4.4%
California	0.0	20.0	0.0	36.6	37.1	4.4
Texas	11.1	20.0	16.7	26.7	14.8	0.0
Other	0.0	20.0	16.7	26.7	18.5	13.0
Unknown	22.2	20.0	66.6	10.0	29.6	78.2
Number	18	5	18	30	27	22

by migrants from Texas, together comprising roughly two-thirds of the sample. In the "Getting By" category, 37 percent were from California and 15 percent were from Texas (yielding a total of 52 percent). In the category "Finding One's Way," however, U.S. destinations were evenly distributed.

Remarkably, retablos that touched on the theme of homecoming generally did *not* mention specific U.S. place-names: 78 percent of these retablos were coded as destination unknown. This high figure reflects the isolation of migrants from their family members. A majority of the homecoming retablos were left by parents, sisters, or brothers, not the migrants themselves, and these people frequently do not know the exact whereabouts of their loved ones until they actually return, and then often only vaguely.

6

▼▼▼

MASTERPIECES ON TIN: A SURVEY OF MIGRANTS' RETABLOS

t is neither feasible nor desirable for us to present all 124 of the votive works that we assembled in our five-year search for migrants' retablos. Not only would the cost of color reproduction be prohibitive, but the pictures vary greatly in quality and there is considerable repetition within subject categories. We therefore selected 40 of the most artistically meritorious works while striving to ensure that all periods, subjects, and images were represented in the catalog. In this chapter, we carry out a detailed interpretive analysis of these selected "masterpieces on tin" (from Giffords 1974).

The frequency distribution of the 40 retablos according to various characteristics is shown in Table 6.1. Forty-five images are mentioned among the ex-votos we selected. As in the full sample, the image most frequently addressed is the Virgin of San Juan de los Lagos, constituting 60 percent of all citations, followed by el Señor de la Conquista with 11 percent, and the Virgin of Guadalupe with 7 percent. Images of el Señor de la Misericordia, el Niño de Atocha, and San Miguel were each mentioned twice, yielding a relative frequency of 4.4 percent. Images of el Señor del Saucito, el Señor de Villaseca, and San Martín de Terreros were mentioned only once apiece (about 2 percent).

Table 6.1. Distribution of Retablos Reproduced in this Volume by Image of Supplication, Subject Matter, and Period of U.S. Migration

	Number	Percentage		Number	Percentage
Image of Supplication			Period of U.S. Migration		
Virgen de San Juan de los Lagos	27	60.0%	The Early Years	5	12.5%
Señor de la Conquista	5	11.1	The Bracero Era	12	30.0
Virgen de Guadalupe	3	6.7	The Growth Years	6	15.0
Señor de la Misericordia	2	4.4	The Modern Era	6	15.0
El Niño de Atocha	2	4.4	Period Not Specified	11	27.5
San Miguel	2	4.4	Mexican Origin		
Virgen de Talpa	1	2.2	Guanajuato	14	35.0
Señor del Saucito	1	2.2	San Luis Potosí	3	7.5
Señor de Villaseca	1	2.2	Other	3	7.5
San Martín de Terreros	1	2.2	Unknown	20	50.0
Total Images Shown	45	100.0%	U.S. Destination		
Subject of Retablo			California	8	20.0%
Making the Trip	9	22.5%	Texas	11	27.5
Finding One's Way	2	5.0	Border	3	7.5
Legal Problems	4	10.0	Other	4	10.0
Medical Problems	8	20.0	Unknown	14	35.0
Getting by in the U.S.	11	27.5	Total Retablos Examined	40	100.0
Homecoming	6	15.0			
Gender of Supplicant					
Male	21	52.5%			
Female	16	40.0			
Unknown/Both	3	7.5			

The 40 retablos are fairly evenly distributed among the major content categories. The one exception is "Finding One's Way," which comprises only 5 percent of the retablos presented, reflecting its low frequency in the full sample; 10 percent of the retablos cover legal problems; 15 percent treat homecoming themes; 20 percent deal with medical problems; 23 percent fall into the category of making the trip; and 28 percent discuss getting by in the United States. As in the complete sample, males predominate slightly among the votaries. Among those whose sex could be assigned, 55 percent were males and 45 percent were females.

All periods are represented in the subsample, with percentages ranging from 13 percent in the early period and 15 percent in the growth and modern eras, to 30 percent in the Bracero period. Approximately 28 percent of the 40 retablos were undated. These frequencies are again similar to those prevailing in the full sample. In addition, as in the original sample, Mexican origins are dominated by the state of Guanajuato, mentioned in 35 percent of the texts, with a large share (50 percent) being classified as origin unknown. Among U.S. destinations, the most frequently mentioned places were in Texas (28 percent) and California (20 percent), with a substantial plurality (35 percent) in the unknown category.

▼

Making the Trip

Migration to the United States is an old and well-established tradition in western Mexico, going back to the turn of the century and even before. A 1906 government report, for example, stated that in Teocaltiche, Jalisco, few laborers were available for local employment "because many . . . had emigrated to the United States" (Archivo Histórico de Jalisco 1906). In the following year, a newspaper from the state of Michoacán reported that "in spite of difficulties suffered at the border, emigration from this district has not ceased . . . so that each day groups of three or four people book passage at stations of the central railroad" (*El Heraldo de Zamora* 1907).

In 1910 authorities in the state of Guanajuato were notified by officials in Chihuahua, a border state, that "they had registered among emigrants in Ciudad Juárez, 1,606 Mexican citizens who were going toward the United States, noting that of this number 697 individuals were from their state." The officials requested that authorities in Guanajuato act to impede "the said immigration and make public the grave difficulties that confront Mexicans in the republic to the north" (Archivo Histórico de León 1910).

More than anything else, it was the railroad connection between Mexico and the United States, completed in 1884, that cemented the link between labor supply and demand that has united the two countries ever since (Cardoso 1980). The growth and spread of the railroads began the first wave of emigration to the United States shortly after 1890, and the flow northward quickened markedly during and after World War I.

Over the years, thousands of Mexicans have worked putting down tracks and maintaining rail beds throughout the United States. With their arrival, employers no longer had to rely on tenuous labor flows from distant countries such as China or Japan. As neighbors, Mexicans could be recruited readily when needed and let go during slack periods with little or no cost to the employer.

Tivurcia Gallego was probably visiting a railroad worker, most likely her husband, when she narrowly escaped death near the small town of Daingerfield, Texas, located on the rail route between Dallas and Texarkana (see fig. 1). On January 24, 1917, she and her small son were walking along the track when, as she crossed a narrow bridge, she was overtaken unexpectedly by a work crew driving a handcar. "Being unable to move to either side, she invoked the Holiest Virgin of San Juan and suffered nothing more than a few blows, and the little boy no more than a glancing blow, having freed himself from greater danger. In thanksgiving she dedicates this retablo."

This painting offers an excellent example of the classic retablo of thanksgiving, the simplest and most common form of votive painting. Señora Gallego and her son kneel reverently before the image of the Virgin of San Juan, who appears suspended in clouds in the upper left corner of the picture. The lines on the brown floor, apparently brick or tile, form an awkward perspective that ends in a flat, blue-green wall, creating the impression of an interior scene.

Rather than attempting to depict the accident itself, an involved artistic task that could double or triple the price of a painting, Doña Tivurcia chose only to show herself and her son devoutly offering thanks to the Virgin for saving them from serious injury during the railway mishap. As is common among migrants' retablos, the text is full of misspellings, lapses in punctuation, and the U.S. place-name is written as a Spanish phonetic approximation of the English word. The Anglicism *puchicarro* (a transliteration of "pushcar") confirms the migrant origins of the donor, who obviously was familiar with the colloquial terminology of railroad workers.

The next retablo relates the story of Juan Luna, who was heading north through the border state of Tamaulipas (probably aiming for the border-crossing point at Matamoros-Brownsville) when he became annoyed with his traveling companions and struck out on his own (see fig. 2). Apparently he got lost in a deep wood and knocked on the door of an isolated house at 10:00 P.M. to ask for help or lodging, but he was mistaken for a bandit by the owner, who brandished a rifle and threatened to kill him. The danger was so great that not only did Señor Luna invoke the Virgin of San Juan, but also St. Martin of Terreros for good measure.

Although the retablo is dated 1942, the clothing worn by the protagonist is reminiscent of an earlier time. Juan Luna wears garments typical of poor campesinos in the 1920s or 1930s: loose-fitting white trousers, a pullover white shirt, and a brown sombrero; the pants and shirt were probably made of cotton and the sombrero of straw (see Redfield 1930; Toor 1947). Over his shoulder he carries a sack that no doubt contains his traveling provisions.

The next series of retablos take up the issue of border crossing, which can be a very hazardous and risky enterprise (see Samora 1971; Conover 1987; Siems 1992). Along much of the border, crossing involves fording the Rio Grande, which in rainy times can rise to considerable depths with treacherous currents. In other places it requires traversing hot deserts without food or water; and in addition to these natural hazards, migrants must also negotiate numerous man-made obstacles.

Every year dozens of migrants are struck by cars on U.S. freeways near the border. Along California's Interstate 5, for example, the problem became so serious that state highway officials were forced to post yellow hazard signs to warn passing motorists of the danger. The signs contain black silhouettes of a father, mother, and child holding hands and darting across traffic, meaning, in effect, "Illegal Alien Crossing." Indeed, one photographic votive we saw (but did not include in the sample) gave thanks to the Virgin of Zapopan "for the miracle of not having been hit on Interstate 5."

The border zone has become a no-man's-land of bandits and vigilantes in recent years, and in many ways the "normal" risks of arrest, detention, and deportation are the least of the migrants' worries. Far more serious are the risks of robbery by criminals, rapes by predatory gangs, or beatings by North American vigilantes upset with the entry of so many "wetbacks" into the United States.

Given these dangers, it is not surprising that migrants who do manage to cross the border safely are deeply grateful and express this gratitude with a votive of thanks dedicated to their favored icon. Figure 3 presents one such example, dated February 2, 1960, and prepared by José Cruz Soria of San Miguel de Allende, Guanajuato, who gave "infinite thanks to our Lady of San Juan de los Lagos for having enabled me to cross the border and return with health."

The painting shows Señor Cruz and a woman, most likely his wife, kneeling on the brown earth before an orange background; the two figures hold votive candles and look away from the viewer into the distant blue sky where the Virgin of San Juan rises within a garland of clouds over a tier of dark mountains. A churning green band divides the upper and lower segments of the painting and probably represents the Rio Grande river. Metaphorically, the retablo probably shows the Virgin of San Juan guiding José Cruz Soria through a dangerous passage into the promised land of good jobs and high wages.

Judging from the primitive quality of its execution, figure 4 was most likely prepared by the donor himself rather than a professional retablo painter. Together with five friends, Amador de Lira overcame a threat to his well-being while crossing the Rio Grande into the United States. In gratitude, he extended "the most infinite thanks for the miracle of saving them as they crossed the dangerous river in Texas." Although the Virgin of San Juan is not identified by name, her image appears in the upper left-hand corner flanked by cherubic angels who hold the Virgin's ribbonlike banner over her head, a standard depiction.

In addition, the painting shows six figures fording the river in single file at the head of a rushing cascade. Each migrant is clearly identified by his initials, and the donor (ADL) is the third figure from the left. Four of the men wear sombreros, while two sport baseball caps, suggesting that the undated picture is of relatively recent origin. Five of the men carry buckets, parcels, or pails in their hands (probably containing shoes, dry clothes, and a few personal items) while one man carries a bag over his shoulder. It is as if they are heading off to work, which in a very real sense they are.

Quite likely Amador de Lira feared losing his footing and being swept down the cataract and drowning in the dark, swirling waters. A sense of sinister danger is communicated by the dark tone of the painting, which depicts the men crossing into a gloomy woods (in fact, most of the Rio Grande passes through a landscape of desert, fields, and canyons).

Crossing the "dangerous river" is especially risky for poor campesinos because many don't know how to swim. One ex-voto described to us by a colleague, Patricia Arias, and dated 1988, expressed the thanks of Socorro Juárez to the Virgin of San Juan de los Lagos "for having saved me when I fell, seeking to cross the Rio Grande, and that I came out well." Another votive in our possession but not presented here expresses the gratitude of Lino Salas and 13 friends, who "went to the Rio Grande near some rapids looking for a way to cross into el norte in search of work, when finding themselves in distress, they exclaimed to the Holy Child of Plateros and give infinite thanks for the miracle of July 28, 1947."

As the latter date suggests, the crossing of the Rio Grande is a very old theme in Mexican votive painting. In a retablo presented by Giffords (1991) four migrants give thanks to the Virgin of Guadalupe "for having saved them from the dangerous episode that occurred on August 25, 1920, upon crossing from Laredo, Mexico, to Laredo, Texas." The picture shows four men in a small rowboat attempting to cross a raging river at flood stage. The churning waters have swept trees from the banks and capsized other boats; the man in the bow desperately reaches out for a shrub on the U.S. bank in a frantic effort to pull the boat ashore.

We have a similar retablo from the same period in our sample (see fig. 5). While attempting to ford the Rio Grande near El Paso, Texas, on May 28, 1929, Domingo Segura apparently lost his footing, fell into the water, and was in danger of being swept downstream to a sure death. In a panic, he desperately invoked the Virgin of San Juan de los Lagos and, as Señor Segura tells it, "At that moment my salvation came from a friend who, bravely fighting the fearful waters, was able to pull me to the river bank. In thanksgiving for so apparent a miracle, I make public the present retablo."

The colorful painting shows the river's blue waters rushing through the arches of a stone bridge to the left. In the center of the composition the hapless Señor Segura flounders in the rapids with his arms raised desperately above his head. From the right of the frame his friend swims against the current to his aid. The Virgin of San Juan is shown floating under her banner in the upper right corner of the picture.

Naturally, most retablos commemorate successful crossings and good fortune; but sometimes they acknowledge sadder outcomes in which luck ran out. One such retablo, reported to us by another colleague who saw it in San Juan de los Lagos in 1982, offered a mother's thanks to the

Virgin for the recovery of the bodies of her two sons, who drowned while trying to cross the Rio Grande into the United States.

Although drowning is a serious risk for migrants seeking to cross into Texas, those planning to go to Arizona, California, or New Mexico face a different hazard: dying of thirst in a lonely desert. Braulio Barrientos of Rancho Palencia, Guanajuato, faced this possibility when he and three companions tried to "re-emigrate" to the United States through the desert and their water supply ran out (see fig. 6). "Traveling in such great heat and with such thirst, and without hope of drinking even a little water, we invoked the Virgin of San Juan and were able to arrive at our destination and return to our homeland in health."

The accompanying picture is remarkably well executed, with a fine attention to detail, light, and perspective. The upper half of the picture is dominated by a searing sun bearing down relentlessly upon four men from a cloudless blue sky. They are crossing a high desert, as indicated by the cacti, scrub bushes, and snow-capped peak in the background. The hot sun spreads a yellow glow on the desert floor, casting long shadows from the men withering in the heat.

In the right half of the composition, one man sits exhausted on the sand with his empty water jug and stares blankly at the viewer. Next to him another holds his dry container dejectedly and fixes his gaze at the sand baking before his eyes. On the left side of the picture, two men look skyward expectantly at an apparition of the Virgin of San Juan, who floats resplendently on a garland of clouds and will guide them to safety. The gold of her cape, pedestal, and banner reflect brilliantly in the bright desert light.

In addition to risks of nature, migrants without documents face one additional, very human hazard: the threat of arrest and deportation by agents of the U.S. Border Patrol. Over the years, the technological arsenal deployed to curb the influx of undocumented migrants has grown increasingly sophisticated, including infrared scopes, remote sensors, radio-dispatched vehicles, and helicopters. One can only imagine the fright and apprehension of rural Mexicans facing the prospect of making their way through the massive hardware.

Figure 7 conveys the sense of relief felt by those who undergo the ordeal successfully. In this retablo, María Esther Tapia Picón gives thanks to the Virgin of San Juan on behalf of herself and two others "for saving us from the migration authorities on our way to Los Angeles." The desert scene and reference to Los Angeles suggests the crossing probably occurred in San Diego

County, the busiest immigration district in the United States. Although unidentified, the women's companions are probably relatives, most likely a husband and daughter or brother and sister.

The picture shows three people in the foreground cowering behind a small bush, hiding from two immigration officers who confer next to their van some distance away; a third officer sits in the driver's seat. The van is radio equipped and the officers appear to be carrying billy clubs. A helicopter with a bright searchlight flies overhead, and a surreal city (San Diego or, metaphorically, Los Angeles) is suspended in clouds just above the horizon, as if it were a mirage. The Virgin of San Juan floats in a nimbus in the upper left corner of the retablo, with two cherubs holding her golden banner aloft.

Interpretation is rendered somewhat ambiguous by several elements of the scene. Although the text clearly refers to "migration authorities" that seek to prevent the supplicant's passage to Los Angeles, the officers in question seem to be on the Mexican side of the border. The van has a Mexican flag painted on its side and there is an apparent border-crossing point on the horizon to the right. These depictions are confusing because Mexican immigration authorities generally do not seek to apprehend people as they enter the United States, and they do not deploy helicopters along the border.

Although migrants report unpleasant encounters with the Mexican border police, these usually occur upon return after a season of work in the United States, when they come back laden with gifts and cash for relatives. Until the government began an extensive clean-up effort in 1989 called Programa Paisano, returning migrants were an all-too-common target for extortion by corrupt customs officials and border police, and even after this clean-up effort the abuses have not been completely eliminated.

In the present case, the protagonists appear to have undertaken evasive actions to circumvent authorities from both nations—Mexican police on the ground and U.S. Border Patrol agents in the air—making the experience all the more harrowing. Whoever the "migration authorities" were, Esther Tapia felt sufficient gratitude to acknowledge the crossing with a retablo to the Virgin of San Juan de los Lagos.

Risks such as drowning, thirst, and apprehension confront anyone who attempts to cross the Mexico-United States border without documents, but if the migrant happens to be a woman, there is the additional risk of sexual assault. For this reason, families are reluctant to let female relatives travel north by themselves or to cross the border unaccompanied (Reichert 1979; Massey et al. 1987). At times, however, circumstances compel a woman to head north by herself. Causes of such migration include widowhood, abandonment, or the loneliness that arises from an extended separation from one's husband. Whatever the reason, the journey is fraught with hazards, as the next retablos indicate.

It is not clear where the occurrence described in figure 8 took place. In her painting, Concepción Zapata gives thanks to the Virgin of San Juan from saving her from a "Texan" who attempted to carry her off in 1948, for what evil purposes we can only imagine. The event could have occurred in the United States, where the "Texan" would have been a North American, or it might have occurred in Mexico, where the "Texan" would have been a Mexican with migrant experience in Texas. In any event, the woman escaped her pursuer by hiding behind a tree with her little brother. The fact that the tree was along a highway suggests that she was on her way northward.

Although Señorita Zapata's painting is basically executed as a simple votive of thanks, with the donor kneeling in gratitude before the holy image, the use of theater motifs underscores the drama of the event and gives the picture considerable artistic interest. Concepción Zapata presents herself on a brightly lit stage holding a votive candle and walking on her knees toward the Virgin of San Juan, who floats in from stage left suspended in clouds. The plush red curtain fastened on the right has just been pulled back to reveal the action under way. The protagonist is thrown into relief by a spotlight that, judging from the shadow it casts, comes from above and behind the viewer's left shoulder. The woman is fully made up, with carefully arranged blonde hair, a green sweater, and a matching plaid skirt. The total effect is to make the viewer feel as though he or she is sitting in the middle row of a theater, about halfway back, looking down upon the action occurring on stage.

In figure 9, references to the problems of Elifonsa Durán, like those of Concepción Zapata, are somewhat obscure. After she went to the United States, her mother learned that she was "delicate" and prayed to the Virgin of San Juan that "they" should stop bothering her and that she should return safe and sound. It is not clear who "they" were or how they were bothering young Elifonsa. She may have been propositioned for sexual favors at work, sexually harassed by her boss, or pestered by unwanted advances from a friend or neighbor. Whatever the problem, it was serious enough that her mother turned to the Virgin of San Juan for help and felt obliged to acknowledge her intercession with a retablo.

The painting indicates that events worked out well and that Elifonsa ultimately returned "con bien" (with well-being). The composition presents mother and daughter kneeling in thanksgiving before an image of the Virgin with votive candles in their hands. The icon appears above them in the right-hand corner of the picture resting on a small cloud. The act of thanksgiving by the two women occurs in no particular place; the gray featureless plain on which they kneel blends into a reddish brown atmosphere—as at dawn or sunset—that eventually gives way to blue sky and wispy white clouds. The figures are rendered in some detail, with each finger on the women's hands delicately outlined.

Another retablo not reproduced here, but one bearing directly on women's issues, refers to "some difficulties" that Serafina Magaña had with her husband, "Mr. Forayt." After entrusting herself to el Señor del Saucito, the problems ceased, and she commissioned a retablo of thanks. "Mr. Forayt" is clearly a misspelled English name, perhaps Forsythe. Señora Magaña's husband might have been a North American who came to Mexico in search of a compliant wife of humble origins whom he could exploit, an all too common occurrence.

In Mexico, unfortunately, there is an informal industry of "mail order brides" and arranged marriages in which older U.S. men take young Mexican wives willing to become subservient spouses in exchange for a U.S. visa and a higher material standard of living. Before "Mr. Forayt" and his bride could return to the United States, however, Doña Serafina had apparently had enough and turned to el Señor del Saucito for help. That the marriage did not last very long is suggested by the fact that in the retablo Señora Magaña does not take her husband's last name, does not know how to spell it correctly, and in the text addresses him using the formal English title "Mister."

Finding One's Way

It is one thing to cross the border into the United States; it is quite another to arrive safely at one's destination and find a job. An address in a pocket or a telephone number on a scrap of paper are sometimes all that a migrant has to find his or her way in the new land, and sometimes not even that. Over the years, countless migrants have gotten lost looking for work, a relative, or some obscure meeting point; and some have disappeared entirely, never to be heard from again.

At the turn of the century, it was common to find classified ads placed in U.S. and Mexican newspapers by desperate people looking for family members who had simply disappeared, either in the United States or on their way northward, leaving relatives in a state of great anxiety and doubt. In the July 16, 1897, issue of *El Correo de Jalisco*, for example, the following announcement appeared: "Mrs. Antonia Ramírez seeks information on the whereabouts of her brother Jesús Ramírez, who in the year 1888 took a trip to the United States on the northern border of the country. The aforementioned person requests, by this means, the reproduction of this notice in newspapers of the border states and Texas" (see Durand 1991).

Getting lost does not always end with grim results. Figure 10 tells the story of Señor Isidro Rosas Rivera, a campesino from a small hamlet near San Luis de la Paz, in the state of Guanajuato. In 1976 he struck out for Texas in search of work with no particular idea where he was going, and after crossing the border, probably near Piedras Negras, Coahuila, he made his way to the small Texas town of Brackettville, about 15 miles from the border, where through sheer luck he found a job on a ranch.

That this "miracle" exceeded his expectations is suggested by the fact that he felt compelled to acknowledge it with a retablo to the Virgin upon his return. The votive painting shows a wooden shed with the front door opened wide to reveal an empty interior. The structure is silhouetted against a blue sky with faint white clouds. A nearby fence and gate suggest that the viewer is standing in the middle of a corral and looking into a stable, no doubt the very place where Señor Rosas worked. To the left, the migrant kneels on the dirt in the barnyard before an image of the Virgin of San Juan de los Lagos, who, on her pedestal suspended in a wreath of clouds, is flanked by golden angels. The great affection Señor Rosas feels toward the Virgin for the "miracle" he received is suggested by his use of the diminutive "Virgencita" (little Virgin) to address the image.

The miracle that was bestowed on Matías Lara of San Luis Potosí did not involve finding a job, but he was no less grateful to the Virgin of San Juan for helping him find his way (see fig. 11). "On November 18, 1919, finding myself lost in Chicago I entrusted myself to the Virgin of San

Juan de los Lagos asking that she illuminate the road that I sought. I give her thanks for granting me what I asked, and for this reason dedicate the present retablo as a memento."

This painting employs a technique common in Mexican votive painting—that of segmenting and rearranging time. To the left of the composition Señor Lara, dressed in his best overalls and with his sombrero at his side, is shown at the moment of supplication, kneeling on a tile floor before an image of the Virgin of San Juan. Although the image of the Virgin is actually only 20 inches tall, in this scene she towers over Señor Lara with a golden glow.

To the right we see Chicago at the time that Don Matías was lost. The viewer looks in toward the city from a viewpoint somewhere in Lake Michigan as buses, or perhaps trams, rush by on Lake Shore Drive. Behind the roadway, a panorama of tall buildings rises up darkly; and although Chicago is located on a flat prairie, in the supplicant's imagination hills loom in the background.

The composition suggests the fright experienced by a poor peasant from a small, rural town who finds himself lost in a giant industrial metropolis. The trepidation caused by such a situation is well-described by Taylor (1932:68), who relates the story of a migrant from Arandas, Jalisco, who also found himself lost in Chicago about the same time as Matías Lara:

> In 1923 I went to San Antonio where I worked for the Southern Pacific. Soon a Friend working at the Inland Steel Company in Indiana Harbor sent me $100 and told me to come there. I reached Chicago, but could find no one who knew where Indiana Harbor was. I knew no English and for six days I was in Chicago, trying to find Indiana Harbor. I got onto street cars, and asked the conductors, but they said, "This car does not go to Indiana Harbor." I would ride a long time, hoping to see Indiana Harbor and then get off and take another car. I couldn't order in restaurants so I couldn't get anything to eat except in stores with some fruit which I could see and point to. At night I slept in box cars, or any place; I couldn't go to a hotel because I didn't know how to ask for a room. I'm scared of policemen, and I didn't think I would stay so long in Chicago, so I didn't ask them. I saw people with dark faces and asked them, but they couldn't understand Spanish. In all that time I saw no Mexican. Finally, in a railroad station I found a man who spoke Spanish; he was a Cuban. He took me to the place to get my train to Indiana Harbor.

Cities are not the only places where a migrant can get lost, as Manuel Chávez can attest. While traveling with two companions he became lost in open country near Needles, California, an agricultural town along the border with Arizona (retablo not included). After wandering for three days, the Virgin of San Juan de los Lagos intervened to save them "from death from hunger and thirst in the desert."

Although the event occurred in 1947, Señor Chávez only got around to acknowledging his debt to the Virgin in 1989. To fulfill a charge after so many years suggests the profound nature of the trauma he must have suffered: even after 42 years, the impression remained a vivid memory and obviously represented a critical experience in his life.

▼

Legal Problems

In order to enter the United States legally, a prospective migrant must somehow obtain a visa from a U.S. consular official. As the demand for immigrant visas has grown and the supply has dwindled, this process has become more and more difficult, and every day long and seemingly endless lines of hopeful migrants form at U.S. consular offices in Mexico City and Guadalajara. To poor applicants, the paperwork requirements seem daunting, and the receipt of a visa often appears to be a true "miracle" requiring acknowledgment to a sacred image.

Figure 12 presents a rather unusual occurrence among votive paintings—a request to a holy image for a specific intercession before the fact rather than an expression of gratitude afterward. In this votive painting, Juan Sánchez asks el Señor de la Conquista to intervene to help him "resolve a problem of arranging some papers of importance in the U.S.A." The desperation of the request is suggested by the scene of supplication, which is painted in black and white. Señor Sánchez appears kneeling on a floor of gray tiles whose lines extend back to meet a blank white wall. He wears black jeans and a gray shirt, and his arms are outstretched, as though beseeching the holy image for help.

The only color in the painting surrounds the holy image of el Señor de la Conquista, who appears in a swirling mass of blue clouds wearing a golden loincloth. From his pink flesh, crimson streams of blood flow from wounds in his ribs, knees, hands, and feet, and sanguine rivulets run down his face from the crown of thorns. The contrast between the vivid color of the image and the dreary black-and-white scene of supplication expresses the great hope that Señor Sánchez places in the powers of the image, known colloquially as "the Lord of Miracles".

Given the retablo's date, November 20, 1990, it is quite likely that the "papers of importance" are part of a request for amnesty under the Immigration Reform and Control Act of 1986. During 1987 and 1988, more than 2 million Mexicans applied for legalization under this law, and by 1990 the last of their cases was being adjudicated. Perhaps Señor Sánchez was worried because he had not yet heard the final outcome of his case, or maybe he had been denied legalization in a preliminary hearing and was awaiting the outcome of an appeal, or perhaps he had been told that his file was incomplete and needed additional documents before legal residence could be granted.

In the wake of the amnesty program, shrines throughout western Mexico were flooded with votive materials touching on problems of documentation. Usually the votives thanked an image of Christ or the Virgin for the "miracle" of legalization. For poor Mexican migrants, the U.S. government's sudden granting of legal residency on such a massive scale was an unexpected gift that was widely perceived to be miraculous, and as a consequence facsimiles of legalization permits and resident visas poured into altars and shrines.

In one votive we photographed for this study but have not reproduced here, a grateful votary fastened a copy of his brother's new "green card" to a retablo and thanked the Virgin for her intercession. In another (also not included), an entire family affixed copies of their legalization cards and wrote a text thanking the Virgin of San Juan "for having conceded us the miracle we asked for" and for "granting us that which we lacked to complete our papers."

Although issues pertaining to documentation have become increasingly prominent in recent years, Mexican migrants have other encounters with U.S. authorities that go beyond the merely bureaucratic. The most pressing worry facing undocumented Mexican migrants in the United States is, of course, the possibility of apprehension by immigration authorities. The risk is greatest during border crossing and drops considerably once one is inside the United States; but fear of *la migra*, as Border Patrol agents are called, never really dissipates.

A deportation is not merely unpleasant and stigmatizing, it is also highly disruptive. Sometimes parents are arrested in a factory raid while their children are at school, leaving the latter uncared for and teachers and school administrators wondering what happened. Moreover, after a deportation, making one's way back to the United States requires an additional expenditure of time and money, and a sudden absence from work may lead an employer to hire someone else. A narrow escape from la migra therefore brings a real sense of relief.

One grateful migrant, whose 1973 brush with la migra was too close for comfort, thanked el Señor de Villaseca "for having made me the miracle that the Immigration didn't catch me in the State of Texas, they being nearly in front of me and me not having my papers in order." The colorful painting, which we have not reproduced here, shows a bucolic scene of rolling hills and green fields through which a roadway passes, lined on either side by a white rail fence. In the distance the migrant, operating a large red tractor, plows the fields. On the highway, a border patrol car, distinctively painted in black and white, has stopped to scrutinize the fields searching for "illegals." Apparently the agents did not consider the operator a suspect, for he wasn't questioned, an oversight for which the migrant was extremely grateful.

Migrants are not always so lucky. In figure 13, Victoriano Grimaldo offered a votive to the Virgin of San Juan to acknowledge the favor of "granting me the miracle of leaving prison in the U.S.A." To the left we see a lonely figure peering out from a barred window set within a white building with a pitch black door. The jailed figure is obviously the supplicant, and the black door symbolizes the dark and endless abyss into which he has figuratively fallen; his only hope is a miraculous intercession by the Virgin of San Juan.

Rather than looking out upon a prison courtyard, however, Señor Grimaldo gazes upon a scene reminiscent of the lush landscape around his native city of San Felipe during the rainy season. Green hills rise up to meet a deep blue sky graced by white cirrus clouds; green trees surround an adobe building, and the brown earth is covered by a patchwork of green plants painted with yellow highlights. Amidst this scene of pastoral tranquility, Señor Grimaldo kneels to present a candle to the Virgin. Rather than floating in the sky, she sits on the brown earth and towers over the migrant. In symbolic terms, the retablo shows the supplicant looking out of jail to a future when he will be in Mexico thanking the Virgin for his freedom.

Figure 14 displays another variation on the theme of imprisonment; however, this time the retablo was prepared to request freedom, not acknowledge it. Juan José Sánchez was still languishing in a U.S. prison in October 1990 when he arranged for a friend or relative to offer his retablo of supplication to el Señor de la Conquista, asking "that he allow them to give me my liberty in the United States."

The picture space is divided in half. To the right the supplicant is shown looking out of an empty jail cell whose white bars and blue interior are set into a jet black background, suggesting the void of despair that presently surrounds him. On the left side, the image of Christ floats in a billowing cloud set against a deep blue sky, representing the only hope to which the poor man can turn.

The last painting dealing with legal issues is shown in figure 15. Although its date cannot be determined, its poor condition suggests that it is very old. Even though it is in bad repair, however, its luminous colors and complex construction suggest that it was impressive when first painted. The text is partially unintelligible but clearly indicates that the donor was arrested by American authorities, imprisoned, and ultimately released, after how long we do not know.

The retablo presents four separate moments of time. In the top middle section, we see the migrant being arrested, along with his "Texan" companions. In the top right corner, he is shown being incarcerated in a castlelike prison flying a U.S. flag overhead. The bottom panel shows a woman, probably the prisoner's mother or wife, kneeling and offering a votive candle to an image that is hidden from view; behind her is a man, no doubt the migrant, who kneels with a candle. The entire left side of the picture is occupied by the image of the Virgin of San Juan de los Lagos. Thus, the retablo segments and rearranges time, treating the instant of arrest, the moment of imprisonment, the hour of supplication, and the eternal time of the Virgin separately.

▼

Medical Problems

Medical problems constitute the most frequently cited theme among the retablos we assembled for this study. As Giffords (1991:5) has noted, "The covert message of ex-votos, even the recent ones, may be the frightening lack of adequate medical attention." That problems of health should be so prominent among migrants is not surprising given the additional dangers of border crossing, the extra risks of an underground life, and the unusual occupational hazards that people without documents customarily face.

Falling sick far away from family and friends is likely to be particularly alienating, and the recovery of health seems that much more "miraculous" as a result. Figure 16 captures, in compelling artistic terms, the isolation and desperation felt by migrants when they succumb to sickness while working alone in the United States. The left half of the picture shows a migrant, identified only as Bernabé H., lying prostrate with pain in a bunk bed in some lonely corner of a desolate barracks. The roof and front walls have been stripped away to reveal the poor man all by himself in the lower bunk. Where the ceiling should be there is nothing but a blue void. The text states that "finding myself suffering from bad cramps I was confined for days in a sanatorium in Nebraska, U.S.A. Being in such a sad state, I invoked the Lord of Saucito, the Virgin of Guadalupe, and the Virgin of San Juan that they should give me health."

The year 1944 suggests that the migrant was one of the millions of "Braceros" recruited by the U.S. Department of Labor for agricultural work in the United States during World War II (see Galarza 1964; Craig 1971). The gnawing loneliness and sense of desperation experienced by the migrant are symbolized by the starkness of the setting, the empty upper bunk, and the blue void surrounding the scene. The extent of the invalid's despair is indicated by his invocation of three different images, as if no amount of divine help could be too much.

The right half of the picture is empty except for the scene of thanksgiving, in which Don Bernabé kneeling is accompanied by a woman, Catarina V., probably his wife. Both are dressed in formal clothes and hold up votive candles to the holy images that are arrayed above. Directly over the couple are the Virgins of Guadalupe and San Juan de los Lagos, while the image of el Señor del Saucito is placed exactly at the center of the composition, dividing it neatly in half and segmenting the action into two distinct times: the moment of the illness itself and the moment of thanksgiving afterward. The images of Christ and the Virgin of San Juan float in clouds, whereas the Virgin of Guadalupe emerges from an aureola of golden light, a characteristic mode of presentation.

Figure 17 shows an especially well composed votive offered by Paula Martínez of Donna, Texas, "to the Holiest Virgin of San Juan de los Lagos in thanksgiving for the miracle she granted me. She gave health to me and my granddaughter, María Silvia Arévalo, when we found ourselves gravely ill." The woman and girl are presented in portrait style, from the shoulders up, with hands clasped in prayer and looking reverently up toward the Virgin of San Juan, who appears in billowing clouds in the upper left corner of the picture.

The whole work is rendered with great care and considerable detail. The embroidery on the Virgin's gown is intricate and her crescent moon is painted a brilliant white with a face drawn in the style of "the man in the moon." The angels holding the Virgin's banner aloft are rendered in a pinkish color with gray wings, and the Virgin's motto is clearly legible along the ribbon.

Unlike in most retablos, moreover, the faces of the two women are treated with human interest so as to convey actual emotion and personality. They are real people looking reverently toward the Virgin with heartfelt thanks and not just stock figures with stiff attitudes. The girl, in particular, is more youthful looking than her grandmother, in contrast to the usual technique of conveying youth simply by drawing children to be small-scale versions of adults.

In recent years, new methods and materials have become available to retablo artists, who have used them increasingly to construct collages rather than simple paintings. In assembling retablos for this project, we discovered three works by the painter of figure 18, an artist who practiced his trade in the region of los Altos de Jalisco during the 1960s and 1970s. All three retablos are dedicated to the Virgin of San Juan and all fasten a photograph to what would otherwise be a standard votive painting on tin.

In each instance, the photograph is fastened to the upper center of the tin sheet with grommets, the image of the Virgin floats in clouds to the right, and the scene of the miraculous happening is on the lower left. As is typical of this artist's work, the retablo thanks the Virgin for curing the illness of the person whose photograph is affixed above. The work, dated August 27, 1968, gives "thanks to the Virgin of San Juan de los Lagos for having returned health to my grandson, Phillip M. García, in the year 1964, from his grandmother, Dolores R. García."

The two names suggest that the donor, and certainly her grandson, were born north of the border; both follow the North American naming custom of using a middle initial and the father's last name rather than the Mexican convention of using the father's and mother's family names. Also, the boy's first name is written in English as Phillip rather than in Spanish as Felipe. In all likelihood, Señora García journeyed back to San Juan de los Lagos from her home in the United States specifically to commission and deposit the retablo, a hypothesis supported by the four-year lapse between the miraculous event and the presentation of the votive.

The background scene gives the impression of an immense but spartan room. A plain brown floor recedes into space to meet a dull purple wall. The drama depicted on the left side of the picture shows a young boy in blue pajamas lying on a bed covered with white sheets. The bed consists of a simple metal frame quite like those found in hospitals of the 1930s and 1940s. Indeed, it is very similar to the bed drawn by Frida Kahlo in her well-known 1932 painting *The Henry Ford Hospital* (see Herrera 1983). A man, probably the boy's father, stands next to the bed watching over him, and to the right is a nightstand containing a white water pitcher.

On the right side of the retablo, the luminous Virgin floats over the floor, dwarfing the human figures. The clouds on which she rests are painted a rich blue, while the trim of her gown is rendered in yellow, orange, and gold. The crescent moon again has facial features, and it and the gown's brocade are executed in brown. The Virgin's flowing brown hair extends halfway down her back and a golden tiara rests on her head; two fleshy, angelic cherubs with white wings hold up her motto on a white ribbon.

The institutional-style bed drawn in this retablo appears repeatedly in migrants' retablos and seems to have become something of a stock symbol for isolation among people who fall ill in a foreign land; the image was used to advantage by Frida Kahlo in *The Henry Ford Hospital*. Another example appears in figure 19, which relates what happened to Venancio Soriano when he fell ill during a trip to the United States: "While at work in Harlingen, Texas, I contracted a grave illness of the left lung that was thought incurable. I offered to visit the Miraculous Little Virgin of San Juan de los Lagos and bring her this retablo as proof of gratitude for her relief."

The entire surface of the retablo has been covered in a drab, institutional olive green, over which the artist has painted two brown lines to indicate the corner of an interior room, two white curtains, and a white bed made up with white sheets. The only human element in this otherwise sterile scene is an expressionless face that emerges from under the covers to stare blankly upward. The large expanse of the bed accentuates the sadness and isolation of the poor migrant.

In most retablos, sickbed scenes are rendered with vigilant family members gathered around; victims are rarely depicted alone. In the present retablo, however, no other human being is in sight. The victim's sense of utter desolation is underscored by the starkness of the scene, by the fact that the curtains are pointedly drawn to shut out all light from outside, and by the very small size of the Virgin herself. Unlike most renderings of the Virgin of San Juan, the artist has chosen to paint the image proportionally *smaller* than it really is. This understatement suggests that the supplicant's faith was sorely tested by the hospitalization in Harlingen.

Another votive dealing with illness is reproduced in figure 20. In it, Eulalia Ortiz of Modesto, California, "gives thanks to our Lord of Villaseca for having recovered from her sickness." This votive work is unusual in that the text appears on a scroll occupying the right side of the composition. To the left we see the supplicant kneeling before the image of el Señor de Villaseca, who is nailed to the cross and clad in a luxuriant red loincloth with white trim. The seriousness of the woman's illness is suggested by the way that the image comes forth out of a dark void, perhaps alluding symbolically to the woman's return from near death.

A recent and very serious threat to the health of migrants comes from the AIDS epidemic. Lonely men working for long periods in the United States unaccompanied by wives or girlfriends all too frequently turn to prostitutes for solace, and drug use represents a very real hazard for children of Mexican migrants who have settled in U.S. urban areas. Through these avenues, AIDS has been introduced into the Mexican migrant population, and the subject has begun to appear in votive paintings.

In one retablo, deposited on December 4, 1993, a young mother addresses the Virgins of Talpa and Guadalupe on behalf of her husband, Carlos, and young son, Carlitos Jr. (not reproduced here). In her text, she says, "Thank you with all my heart for taking AIDS away from me." It is not clear from the work whether she is grateful because a positive HIV test turned out to be a false alarm, or whether she is HIV positive and is thankful because she did not pass the virus to her husband and son. Whatever the case, we can expect additional retablos treating this theme in coming years as the AIDS epidemic spreads.

Surgery constitutes another health problem frequently encountered in Mexican retablos. Having an operation is always difficult and the prospect raises deep fears among most people, but for poor migrants with a limited command of English, a poor understanding of medicine, and a fear of modern technology, subjecting oneself to the surgeon's scalpel can be truly petrifying. These feelings of apprehension and vulnerability are dramatically captured in figure 21, offered by María de la Luz Casillas and her children, of Los Angeles, California, in August 1961.

The picture shows a woman about to be operated on by two surgeons dressed in white gowns. Their faces are covered with surgical masks and they are assisted by a nurse also clad entirely in white. The patient lies face up on the operating table with arms immobilized at her side and her body covered to the shoulders with a white sheet. The nurse appears ready to hold down her feet while one of the doctors pins down her shoulders. The surgeon holds a pair of scissors above her breast about to plunge them in and begin cutting. Other instruments are laid out on a nearby table.

We have seen several other paintings by the same artist at the Sanctuary of el Niño de Atocha, the earliest from 1961 and the latest from 1988 (although none of these were commissioned by U.S. migrants). The style and composition of the operating scene are always the same, suggesting that placement and attitude of the figures and the wielding of the scissors are developed for maximum psychological effect rather than verisimilitude.

In the present instance the action takes place in a large gray room with no doors, windows, or other people. To the left side of the retablo we see four very tiny figures—the sick woman and her three children—desperately beseeching the Virgin for protection. The image of the Virgin rises resplendently on a cloud surrounded by a brilliant golden aureola.

The text offers thanks to the Virgin of San Juan "for having made me so great a miracle of saving me in a dangerous operation that was performed on me for the second time on the 9th day of October 1960, in Los Angeles, California. Which put me at the doors of death but entrusted to so miraculous a Virgin I could recover my health, for which I make apparent the present retablo: in sign of thanksgiving I give thanks to the Holiest Virgin of San Juan."

The theme of dangerous operations continues in figure 22, offered by Antonia Ramos de González of Oxnard California in 1971. In the lower left corner of the retablo we see Señora González lying on an operating table under a high-beam light that illuminates two masked surgeons wearing white gowns. Beside the table is a tank of compressed gas, presumably the anesthesia. A splotch of red over the prone body indicates the sanguine nature of the procedure under way. The scene is isolated in space and time and completely removed from other visual referents in the composition. Indeed, the image of the Virgin appears in the opposite corner of the retablo in a dark bronze glow, unconnected to the action under way, and the text simply states that "I give infinite thanks to the Holiest Virgin of San Juan because she conceded me my health in a very dangerous operation."

Physical illness is only one risk for Mexican migrants to the United States. The harsh conditions of life, the poor working conditions, the culture shock, and the isolation from friends and family all take their psychological toll. In life histories that have been compiled, migrants uniformly state how difficult the migratory experience can be (see Gamio 1931; Herrera-Sobek 1979;

Massey et al. 1987; Siems 1992). In some cases, they report the strain being so intense that they feel like they are "going crazy" (Gamio 1931).

In one retablo we discovered, reproduced in figure 23, a migrant apparently did "go crazy," becoming so psychotic that he required restraint. The retablo was left on behalf of Angel Ortiz by his worried mother. The text states that upon learning that her son "was very ill in a hospital in the United States, and that they had chained him to a bed because he tried to run away, and that they had bound him by the feet and arms, I invoked the Holiest Virgin of San Juan de los Lagos and the Virgin of Guadalupe in Mexico, D.F., to give him relief."

The retablo is neatly divided into left and right sections by a red border. The left side contains the text and the right side is dominated by a depiction of the Virgin of San Juan, who rises suspended against a background of blue and white clouds with two cherubs holding her golden banner aloft. In the bottom right corner of the frame we see the poor migrant, Angel, his hands and feet tied to the corners of his hospital bed. The mother's deep worry is signalled by the fact that she invokes not one, but two images of the Virgin, and by the fact that the image she shows, the Virgin of San Juan, is drawn many times larger her actual size, suggesting the great hope the mother places in the image's powers.

Angel Ortiz is not the first migrant to experience psychological distress, of course. Indeed, one psychologically disturbed migrant became something of a sensation in the art world during the 1970s and 1980s. Martín Ramírez migrated to the United States from his native Jalisco sometime after the turn of the century, probably during the 1920s. According to his psychiatrist in the United States, Dr. Tarmo Pasto (cited in Longhauser 1985):

> He soon found that in America his life was so different from his life in Mexico that he
> became bewildered. The cultural shock was too much for him. He became disoriented,
> delusional, and had hallucinations, exhibiting all the characteristics of a schizophrenic.
> He was working on the railroad as a section hand, but the work became too demanding on
> his physical energies.

After being picked up by authorities in a Los Angeles park wandering about in a confused state, Ramírez was confined to a mental hospital in 1930, where he spent the next 30 years of his life. Around 1945 he spontaneously began to draw, paint, and create collages using materials he found in the hospital. While he was alive his psychiatrist was his only patron, but in 1968, six years after his death, a Chicago artist named Jim Nutt came across examples of his work while teaching in Sacramento, and together with his gallery dealer, Phyllis Kind, he purchased the corpus of Ramírez's surviving art from the psychiatrist, then about 300 works.

Through their promotional efforts, the pictures of Martín Ramírez became popular among collectors of "outsider" art, a favorite genre for the avant-garde of Chicago, New York, and Los Angeles, and his works ultimately came to fetch prices of $20,000 or more. The pictures blend stylized images of horses, animals, and people from his native region of Jalisco with fantastic images of trains, tunnels, and tracks drawn from his experience as a migrant worker (see McGonigle 1985; Longhauser 1985; Smith 1985; Bowman 1985; Martin 1985; Cardinal 1986).

Although he was not a retablo painter, many of his pictures employ a similar style and draw upon a common set of primitive techniques: the simplification of action to highlights, the naive and highly stylized rendering of human figures, the appearance of images and apparitions, and the fragmentation of time (see Durand 1991).

▼

Getting By in the United States

Once they have crossed the border and achieved a relatively secure foothold in the United States, migrants begin to confront other issues that arise when a brief sojourn lengthens into a stay of months or years. Should a migrant obtain legal documents, he and his children become subject to the requirements of the military draft. All children born in the United States, even of undocumented parents, face the prospect of conscription; and over the years thousands of Mexicans have ended up in theaters of war they scarcely could have imagined when they left their peaceful towns in search of work in el Norte.

The oldest wartime retablo that we located hangs in the sanctuary at Mineral de Cata. Because of its poor condition it is not reproduced here, but it shows a soldier on a World War I battlefield with airplanes streaking overhead and explosions bursting all around. The text, written by the uncle of the soldier, was presented in the last chapter.

Giffords (1974) reproduces a World War II retablo left by Everardo G. de Corral of Salinas,

California, who gives thanks to el Niño de Plateros for saving his son during the battle of Okinawa. The picture shows two men huddled behind a stone wall on a battlefield denuded of all vegetation. As explosions burst all around, one of the two soldiers fires over the wall with his rifle while the other doubles over as he is struck by bullets. In a cartoon bubble the wounded man cries out to the holy image. A dead body lies sprawled at his feet. The text states that Señor de Corral's son

> suffered three wounds in the same day. The first one was in the right side, the second beneath his heart, and the third one in his stomach; the first two wounds were done by a rifle, and the third one with a machine gun. These wounds had him between life and death, but the child Jesus listened to my prayers that I was making in my house for him, and he also listened to my son who used to acclaim him every moment. The Holy Child of Plateros saved him. That is why I and my son give infinite thanks and make public his power. (Giffords, 1974:137)

Figure 24 shows a wartime votive from our sample in which Juanita Limón of Needles, California, gives thanks to el Señor de la Misericordia "for having freed my husband from going to the war in Korea." Although the text makes it sound as though Señor Limón might never have been sent overseas, the picture suggests otherwise. In the top right quadrant we see Señor Limón dressed in full battle gear with helmet, pack, rifle, and bayonet silhouetted against a dark orange sky filled with explosions and diving airplanes. Highlighted along with the protagonist are a tank, a cannon, and another bomb explosion. To the left of the picture, we see Señora Limón kneeling before the holy image with a rosary in her hand. Golden orange light emanates from the center of the cross and blends into the battlefield sky.

Despite its graphic depiction of warfare, it is not clear whether the retablo splits time between the husband's actions on the battlefield and the wife's later thanksgiving, in which case the image's intercession prevented a *return* to the Korean War, or whether it splits time between the wife's supplication and what might have occurred on the battlefield, in which case the image saved her husband from being sent there *in the first place*. Whatever the case, the use of biplanes rather than jet fighters suggests that Señora Limón's mental images of warfare are drawn not from Korea, but from World War I, a symbolic device common in the fine arts and literature as well (see Fussell 1975).

We have two Vietnam-era votives in our sample. The first, not reproduced here, is a collage-style retablo commemorating a miracle that occurred in battle on February 19, 1967. In the upper left corner of the picture, the subject's photograph has been affixed. Below on the battlefield he is painted in uniform with helmet, backpack, and rifle and is falling backward at the moment of his wounding. Across a lifeless gray and brown wasteland, barbed wire stands out in the distance (more World War I imagery). The sky is dark, as if on the edge of a storm, and several shells burst in the air. Out of the largest shell burst, the holy image of the Virgin appears in rays of white light, as if in a vision. In the text, José Luis Palafox "gives thanks to the Holiest Virgin of Zapopan for having protected me and saved my life upon being wounded in combat."

The second Vietnam-era work is dedicated to el Niño de Atocha and was left by Paula Vázquez on behalf of a male relative, probably her son, brother, or husband (see fig. 25). El Niño de Atocha is mentioned by name in the text, but the image does not appear in the painting, the "miracle" being implicit (preserving the life of the soldier during his tour of duty in Vietnam).

Although the text is spare and undated, the painting captures the distinctive nature of combat in Vietnam (see Herr 1978; Baker 1981; Santoli 1981). Four soldiers are on patrol, perhaps on a "search and destroy" mission. They are dressed in battle fatigues and crossing a clearing in single file at twilight or dawn. Their faces have been blackened with camouflage grease, and all carry M-1 rifles. The lead soldier, probably the subject of the retablo, also carries a radio and an ammunition canister slung on his back. He is several paces ahead of the others as he moves toward the viewer away from the jungle in the background.

The composition suggests that the four "grunts" have withdrawn from a firefight after calling in air strikes on the jungle behind them. Two jets streak overhead at treetop level, dropping bombs into the jungle. One bomb explodes just over the horizon to the left of the picture, and an antiaircraft shell bursts in the upper right corner.

In the course of our investigation we encountered many collages on military themes, but none so powerful and affecting as this painting. Usually military votives are not paintings, but photos or texts written on paper. The shrine to the Virgin of San Juan de los Lagos in San Juan, Texas, for example, is covered with pictures of young men in military uniform, each accompanied by a letter of thanks for a promotion, a discharge, a safe return from a tour of duty, and most recently, for surviving the Persian Gulf War.

Less dramatic than the risk of death on the battlefield, but far more frequent and often just as deadly, is the risk of an accident at work. The first retablo on U.S. migration that we ever saw, the one that ultimately led us to undertake this book, dealt with this theme. Although we had no camera at the time and were unable to photograph the picture, we took notes and copied the text carefully.

The retablo showed a United Airlines 747 parked at Chicago's O'Hare Airport. A baggage cart was depicted crashing into the side of the aircraft and the text of Raúl Rodríguez, dated May 28, 1988, stated that while "working as an airplane baggage-handler I had an accident. I hit the plane with a metal cart and made a big hole. I got frightened. At the same moment, I asked the Virgin of San Juan de los Lagos that I would not lose my job. She heard my pleas and nothing happened to me."

Earlier in the century, another migrant feared losing more than his job when he had an accident at work (see fig. 26). "On the 5th day of April of 1908, Gumercindo Ramírez fell from a handcar in Florence, Kansas, U.S.A. It ran over him and broke his ribs, leaving him near death. But as he fell he entrusted himself to the Miraculous Lady of San Juan who saved him, and in proof of this marvelous miracle I dedicate the present memento."

The action appears to occur near dawn just outside a labor camp for railroad employees (see the tent to the far left of the picture). The sky is dark with a faint light behind the hills on the horizon, and trees are silhouetted in the foreground. Railroad tracks run horizontally across the composition, then turn and head backward to infinity. In the center of the picture, we see a railroad handcar that has just come to a stop after running over Señor Ramírez, who lies prostrate below, mangled on the wooden ties between the rails. The men on the handcar are jumping off to attend to the wounded man. In the upper left-hand corner, the Virgin of San Juan rises on a cloud offering her divine protection to the scene of the ghastly accident.

The collage shown in figure 27 deals with the consequences of an accident at work rather than the event itself. When Mexican immigrants work in the United States, they generally have federal and state taxes deducted from their paychecks and often insurance premiums as well, but they don't always receive the benefits to which they are entitled. In order to get an insurance company to pay its claim, at times workers must resort to legal proceedings, a forum in which Mexicans, who often lack legal documents, are at a disadvantage and usually don't expect to win.

Thus, it seemed like a real "miracle" to Marciano Alcocer Castillo when he suddenly received an indemnity check in the mail after being injured on the job: "I had an accident and was injured in the lower back and couldn't work. The insurance company wouldn't recognize my injury and pay what they owed me, so I commended myself to the Holiest Virgin of San Juan, and she gave me the miracle. She made me get better and sent me the check from my accident."

In this retablo the text is placed at the top rather than in its customary location at the bottom of the picture. Don Marciano, wearing black pants, a yellow belt, a blue shirt, and matching blue socks, kneels on a gray floor set against a beige wall. His figure is exceptionally well drawn, with his shirt precisely detailed and his pink face outlined carefully and in fine detail. The work appropriates the collage method by pasting a photo of the Virgin of San Juan within a blue cloud that has been painted in the upper left corner of the retablo to serve as a frame.

Figure 28 offers a convenient transition to our next subject, traffic accidents, because it concerns a vehicle accident that occurred on the job. Senovio Trejo was working in the United States on a cotton farm, probably moving between work sites on the ranch, when "the car broke down and crashed into a light post. It struck me on the head and put me in very great danger far from my homeland and my family." Entrusting himself to San Miguel, however, he recovered and everything apparently turned out all right.

A two-lane road extends from front to back and disappears on the horizon. To either side of the road cotton plants are arranged in symmetrical rows as far as the eye can see. In the distance, mountains rise out of the valley toward a blue sky laced with faint white clouds. About three-quarters of the way down the road we see a vehicle, a jeep, that has just crashed into a utility pole, which leans precariously onto the vehicle. In the foreground a red convertible has just stopped and the passenger is getting out to see what happened.

The retablo is undated, but the style and make of the car suggest that it was painted in the 1950s. In this case, the protagonist was most likely a contract laborer under the Bracero Program, probably doing seasonal work in California's central valley, which in the 1950s was just emerging as an important cotton-growing region. The only other structure in the scene is a shed near the horizon, which represents a barracks used to house migrant farmworkers. To the left the Archangel Michael, with his cape, wings, raised sword, and standard, appears in the sky in a burst of light to save the poor migrant from harm.

Another car accident, unrelated to employment, happened to Manuel and Elena Sánchez as they attempted to negotiate a dangerous curve near El Paso, Texas (see fig. 29). The car in which they were riding left the highway and overturned three times to leave Manuel in a coma for 12 hours without hope of life and apparently beyond the aid of medical science. In desperation, his mother turned to the Virgin of San Juan and as a result, Manuel miraculously awoke without even a headache.

This retablo is unusual in that it is painted on a piece of metal used to fashion license plates. The action is split in time: 1934, when the accident occurred, and 1947, when the retablo was offered. The painting is rendered over a tawny yellow background. Blue clouds swirl over a mountain pass with a road that curves through pine trees between two peaks. By the side of the road is an overturned car, and a legend with an arrow pointing to the crash site saying, "The accident occurred in April 1934." In the bottom left-hand corner we see Manuel Sánchez and his wife on their knees holding up votive candles to thank the Virgin of San Juan thirteen years later; behind them Manuel's mother kneels with her candle. The Virgin, appearing high up in the clouds in the upper right-hand corner of the picture, is drawn in relatively small scale compared to most votive works.

The next votive painting, shown in figure 30, is interesting not only for the drama and color of the events it depicts, but also for what it reveals about urban development in the United States. In this work Angela Chávez thanks the Virgin of San Juan for saving her in 1940 after she was nearly killed in a head-on collision in Los Angeles, California. The crash, between a red farm truck and a blue sedan, forms the central action of the retablo. In the upper left-hand corner of the painting the Virgin emerges out of a light blue sky in a swirl of clouds to offer protection to the accident victim. The skyscrapers of downtown Los Angeles appear over the mountains to the right and suburbs are around the corner of a hill to the left. The incident probably occurred in the San Fernando Valley, which in 1940 still boasted green fields, orchards, and truck farms, but which 50 years later had become a smog-filled part of the city of Los Angeles.

The rural landscape depicted in figure 31, in contrast, probably has not changed much since the work was first painted in 1946. In that year, Jesús Domingo Herrera was hit by a car while walking along the roadside near the small town of Marsing, Idaho. The text states that Señor Herrera came there as a laborer contracted under the Bracero Program, probably living in the encampment of tents shown at the lower left-hand corner of the picture. Vibrant green fields with regular furrows extend back from both sides of a tree-lined roadway that passes from the middle of the composition toward the front right.

On the near side of the roadway by a telephone pole lies the injured body of Señor Herrera. According to the text, "I was walking along a highway when an automobile struck me and dragged me a distance of 20 meters, leaving me senseless." The car that hit him apparently moved on, but still more dangers await the injured migrant as another car and truck approach from around the bend apparently unaware that he is lying unconscious in the roadway. Just in the nick of time, the Virgin of San Juan appears in clouds attended by golden angels to save the poor man from this desperate situation.

Another accident-related retablo is that of Josefina Rivera who in August 1954 fell under the wheels of a bus in Brownsville, Texas (see fig. 32). This retablo is notable for its skillful use of perspective to highlight the drama of unfolding events. The picture is painted from the viewpoint of someone situated just above the center of the intersection. On the cross street going from left to right, Señorita Rivera has fallen off the curb before an oncoming bus, which has just stopped inches from her sprawling body. The eye is drawn to this focal point by the rendering of the perpendicular street, which begins narrowly in the distance and then steadily widens to open up on the fateful intersection. To the left, the Virgin of San Juan sits on her golden pedestal offering her serene protection to the drama unfolding on the right.

Finally, in figure 33 we consider a votive left by J. Cruz Ontiveros, who thanks San Miguel "for granting me the miracle of coming out well from an accident that I had in a pickup truck on the highway in Waxahachie, Texas, U.S.A." Dated September 16, 1972, the picture shows a peaceful country road winding through a landscape of rolling hills and mountains dotted with green trees and verdant pastures. In the distance we see a farmhouse and a windmill.

The picture is divided into two temporal segments. In the center of the picture, where the road crosses a narrow stone bridge as it passes over a small creek, we see the scene of the miraculous event. A white pickup lies overturned by the side of the road and its driver lies prone on the ground beside it, either dead or severely injured. A red pickup truck has screeched to a halt in the roadway apparently unharmed, and its driver, wearing a white shirt, has gotten out to survey the scene of the wreck.

In the foreground, the action shifts to the time of the votive act, and we see the supplicant wearing the same white shirt and kneeling before the image of San Miguel, who stands triumphant with his sword raised over the prostrate figure of Satan. Señor Cruz holds a votive candle in his right hand and his hat is placed reverently against his bent knee. His attitude and positioning suggest the profound gratitude he feels at escaping what must have been a very close call.

In addition to traffic accidents, migration carries one last risk related to the street: crime. Over the years, Mexican migrants have increasingly settled in U.S. urban areas (see Bean and Tienda 1987; Bartel 1989), and being poor, they often find themselves living in dangerous, deteriorated inner-city neighborhoods close to the homes of other poor minority groups. Jesús Gómez seems to have been one of these urban migrants, because his painting (fig. 34) depicts an armed confrontation on the streets of Compton, California, a predominantly black community adjacent to Los Angeles.

In the picture, the protagonist is driving by or toward a bar called La Frontera, whose doors swing open, and his car has just been stopped by two men, apparently African Americans, one brandishing a shotgun. The text is not specific about the nature of the attack, saying only that Señor Gómez gives "thanks to the Lord of Mercy for a favor received" in July 1981. The attack might have been a robbery, a carjacking, a gang attack, or some other criminal action, but whatever its nature Señor Gómez felt it was a miracle that he had survived to tell the story.

▼

Homecoming

The final phase of any trip to the United States is homecoming, an event likely to be met with heartfelt gratitude by migrants and family members alike. Before one arrives in the safety of one's hometown, however, there is the small matter of the journey back from the United States, which itself can be fraught with dangers. Because migrants typically return with goods and cash, they make tempting targets for thieves and unscrupulous officials as they cross the border back into Mexico.

Such was the fate of one unfortunate migrant who journeyed homeward to his "family's side" in 1943 (see fig. 35). As the text explains,

I was coming from the United States of America when, just after crossing the border in Chihuahua, I was assaulted on the train by thieves who wanted to take my life and rob me of the money and all that I carried. But they didn't accomplish their goal thanks to the Holiest Virgin. When the bandit struck at me with a dagger, an impulse made me defend myself with such force that I broke a glass window with my back and fell backwards outside, landing on the ground so hard that I thought for sure I would lose my life. And if this was not enough, the van that picked me up to bring me to the hospital turned over.

The picture shows a train pulled by a steam locomotive belching smoke and charging into the night air, moving away from the viewer toward the upper right corner of the frame. Telegraph wires and poles parallel the tracks on the far side, and a maguey cactus is situated in the lower left, next to the text, which is set off in a special section as if on a plaque. Behind the text is a nopal cactus that is partially obscured.

The action occurs on the left side of the picture where we see the migrant under attack by a man in a dark suit and hat who is attempting to stab him with a dagger. The protagonist has just broken through the glass of the passenger car window and is falling backward toward the ground, to his death or safety he is not sure, but as he falls he invokes the Virgin of San Juan de los Lagos, who appears as a brilliant apparition in the upper right corner, coming forth to save him out of a blinding yellow light in a nimbus of clouds and flanked by attendant angels.

Although the Miraculous Virgin saved him from death in the fall from the train, her protection fell somewhat short later, as the ambulance in which he was riding to the hospital apparently crashed and turned over, adding insult to injury. Nonetheless, the migrant felt extremely grateful to be alive and to have returned to the bosom of his family, and in commemoration he commissioned the colorful retablo.

Periods of the year when migrants return home—especially Christmas—are joyful and full of celebration. Migrants return with gifts for friends and relatives and have plenty of money to spend. Towns that are half empty for most of the year suddenly bustle with activity and fill up with young men hoping to attract the attention of young women who gather nightly in the plaza. Migrants move from house to house drinking, eating, and conversing to catch up on gossip and show off new clothes and possessions. Special parades and masses are held to welcome *los ausentes* (the absent ones), and a series of fairs and rodeos are organized. Townspeople look forward with great anticipation to soccer tournaments featuring migrant players. Priests work overtime to keep up with the demand for marriage ceremonies (see Reichert 1979; Mines 1981; López Castro 1986; Massey et al. 1987).

Figure 36 graphically depicts the great joy experienced by one mother, Candelaria Arreola of El Grullo, Jalisco, at the moment of her son's homecoming in 1955. She stands in the door of their home with arms outstretched to embrace him as he arrives home with a wave of the hand; he is wearing a sombrero, blue pants, and white shirt, and carries a suitcase. The door of their red-roofed home is outlined with red bricks inlaid into the white adobe, creating a pleasing contrast. The Virgin of Talpa floats above in a light blue sky surrounded by white clouds and has a golden halo around her head.

The mother's loneliness, worry, and longing for her son are indicated by the fact that she had begun to say a novena to the Virgin for his return, but before she could finish he miraculously arrived. As she explains, "I give thanks to the Holiest Virgin of Talpa for having brought my son home from the United States, where he stayed for a long time. I began to pray your novena and I hadn't even finished when he returned. Thank you, my Mother!"

Figure 37 offers thanks from both a father and mother for the return of one son from the United States and the healing of another. The father stands with his head bowed reverently in prayer, his arms crossed while holding his hat in his left hand. The mother kneels on the ground and reaches out with emotion to the image of el Señor de la Conquista, who rises above the ground surrounded by rays of golden light. One of the sons stands in the foreground facing the image with his back to the viewer and holding his hat in his hands behind him. His youth is indicated by his small size compared to that of his parents.

The landscape depicts a typical scene from rural Mexico. The brown earth is broken here and there by clumps of green grass; tall, sparsely scattered trees glisten in the afternoon sun as billowing clouds drift by high in a clear blue sky. Gray mountains rise up from the valley floor behind the family's adobe home. The text of thanksgiving was prepared by the father, Francisco Trujillo, for el Señor de la Conquista because "entrusted to him, one son was cured of a strong pain that he suffered in the stomach and the other son reappeared after being lost for some time."

Figure 38 is unusual because it combines acts of thanksgiving and supplication within a single votive work. In the text, a mother and father give thanks to el Señor de la Conquista for healing one son "from an unknown sickness," but at the same time they ask "for the return of my other three sons who are in the U.S., one with his family and the other two bachelors." The order of the names—first the mother María Marcos Rebolloso and then the father Leonardo Arsola— and the use of the possessive adjective *my* suggests the text was written by the lonesome mother.

Two remarkable features of this sophisticated votive painting, created by the same artist as figure 37, are its expert use of perspective and its mixing of time. In the lower right corner of the picture, the two parents kneel on the brown earth before the image of el Señor de la Conquista, who again floats off the ground in a golden glow. As in the previous picture, the woman extends her hands in supplication to the holy image while the father clasps his in silent prayer; their hands nearly come together and appear to be supporting the image of Christ as it floats in the air. The father has removed his hat, which lies against his knee, while the mother's head is covered with a brown shawl.

This act of faith and veneration occurs in the middle of a wide village street seemingly at midday; the deep blue sky and bright white clouds suggest a hot afternoon. To the left of the parents we see three sons, who stand facing the image of Christ at different distances from the viewer. The closest is rendered in exactly the same pose and almost the same colors as the father of Retablo 37, with his head bowed, his arms crossed, and his hat in his hand. The next son stands at attention in a blue shirt and brown pants squarely facing the holy image, as does the third son in the distance. In the background we see a row of adobe houses arranged to form a perspective line that extends back in space to a point on the horizon exactly below the suspended image of Christ.

Although the parents' act of supplication occurs in the present, the rapt and respectful attention paid by the three sons to the left takes place at some date in the future, when they have returned as a result of the miracle to be granted by the holy image. The placement of the figures at different distances from the viewer within a space characterized by a clearly defined receding line of perspective gives the painting an eerie quality, very similar to the effect achieved by surrealist painters such as René Magritte or Salvador Dalí.

Compared to this masterwork of retablo art, the ex-voto of figure 39 appears somewhat crude, but it too contains an element of considerable interest. In this retablo, the mother of a U.S. migrant identified only by the initials F. P. gives thanks to el Señor de la Conquista "for having granted me the miracle of allowing my son to return from the el norte after arranging his papers." The accompanying picture shows the mother and son kneeling in a desert landscape before an image of Christ, which rises up from the desert floor in a white cloud, as if a mirage. In the background, dark mountains stand out against a blue sky with wispy white clouds.

The most distinctive feature of the picture, however, and the element that identifies it instantly as Mexican, is the self-conscious placement of four maguey cactus plants within the landscape. They are arranged so that each figure—Christ, the migrant, and his mother—is confined on either side by the spiked leaves of this distinctive desert plant. With the exception of the nopal cactus, which appears in Mexico's national emblem, the maguey is closest to the Mexican soul, dotting the landscape throughout the central plateau region. It occupies a special place in the heart of Mexicans because from its juice that most characteristic of Mexican beverages, tequila, is created.

The last retablo we present (fig. 40) graphically symbolizes what international migration has become: a tangible and permanent link between the peoples and cultures of Mexico and the United States. In the bottom left-hand corner, the stars and stripes of the U.S. flag form a decorative triangle, while in the lower right-hand corner the Aztec eagle and the distinctive bands of the Mexican flag provide a symmetrical contrast. Between these two ornamental flourishes a text states that "Mrs. Carmen Ortiz commended her husband, Mr. Mateo Hernández, to the Virgin of San Juan de los Lagos, that he should return from the United States after he found himself sick in his eyes. For this they give thanks for her favor."

The painted scene above the text is labeled "retablo"; it shows Señora Ortiz and her husband kneeling on a red brick floor against a featureless blue background. The woman wears a red blouse, white skirt, and dark shawl, and she holds a shining votive candle out in front as she reverently bows her head. The husband kneels behind her wearing a dark jacket and gray pants with hands folded at his waist and with his hat carefully placed by his side. To avoid any confusion, the two figures have been labeled "C. O." and "M. H." The retablo was signed by the artist, Núñez, whose name appears at the end of the text.

The image of the Virgin of San Juan is clad in a white robe embroidered with red flowers. She sits crowned on her pedestal flanked by cherubs who are modestly clad in diapers. The Virgin is surrounded not only by her usual nimbus, but also by a yellow aureola and golden rays of light. She appears to be bursting out of a dark blue atmosphere to bestow a miracle on the couple kneeling to the right, an interpretation that is confirmed by the appearance of the word *milagro* (miracle) in the space between Señora Ortiz and the resplendent image.

▼

Migrants' Retablos in Perspective

The artistic combination of the two national flags in the final votive (fig. 40) embodies in a very simple and elegant way the union of peoples and cultures that is now occurring within the North American continent, a marriage with implications that go far beyond folk art. The use of the two national emblems in a single artistic work dramatizes the ongoing synthesis that for the past 60 years has been forging a new transnational culture born of international movement.

Many studies have documented the remarkable degree to which U.S. migration has been incorporated into the social life of western Mexico (for a review see Durand and Massey 1992). This finding is hardly novel. Most prior works, however, have relied on the standard tools of social science: ethnographic fieldwork, statistical analyses, and case studies, which lead to an abstract understanding that is divorced from the emotional reality of the underlying behavior. Votive paintings provide a more tangible and compelling view of the complex phenomenon of international migration, one that packs considerably more punch than mere statistics.

Retablos reveal unambiguously and unequivocally the degree to which U.S. migration has become a core part of the collective experience of the Mexican people. Working in the United States is now an institutionalized feature of that nation's culture and society. It has been interwoven into the rituals of daily religious life and has itself transformed those rituals. In western Mexico, seeing a retablo signed in Los Angeles, Dallas, or Chicago is as natural as seeing one from Guadalajara, Morelia, or León.

At present, hundreds of thousands of families in western Mexico have a relative on "the other side" and know firsthand about the joys, privations, sorrows, and devotions of migratory life. Migrants customarily maintain close ties with their relatives at home, and while working abroad they dream of returning to build a house, open a store, buy land, or retire in luxury; and if these dreams remain elusive, at least they can look forward to making a visit to the local shrine to pay homage to a venerated image. Each year thousands make such a pilgrimage to appear before images of the

Virgin located in Zapopan, Talpa, and San Juan, or to thank images of Christ in Mineral de Cata, San Luis Potosí, San Felipe, or Plateros.

The retablos we have presented are important because they depict a side of migration usually not told in statistical reports or even in detailed interviews with migrants. Going to el norte has become a rite of passage for young men, synonymous with adventure, excitement, and personal esteem. It represents a source of pride and satisfaction for those who return with goods and money; and success in the United States is a frequent subject of boasts and exaggerated stories. In this atmosphere, those who have not fared well are apt to remain silent. They do not want people to think they were lazy or afraid. Only to a sacred image can they tell the truth and reveal their true stories of sadness, fear, and apprehension.

This book is about these stories and more. Retablos testify to the feelings and experiences of people who migrate back and forth to work in a strange land. As "the one true . . . pictorial expression of the Mexican people," they get at the heart of the matter in a way that academic reports never can. After looking at the pictures presented here, and seeing how deeply migration has become rooted in the popular culture of western Mexico, one intuitively grasps why simply passing a new law or changing a bureaucratic regulation will not and cannot end the ongoing flow of people across the border.

For better or for worse, international migration is pulling Mexico and the United States closer together and blending their peoples and cultures in new and exciting ways. The process of bi-national union is now far too advanced to be controlled by the political and economic leaders who originally set it in motion. Whatever one's feelings about it, the cultural synthesis embodied in these retablos is the way of the future.

7
▼▼▼

CATALOG OF RETABLOS

Retablo of Tivurcia Gallego

▼▼▼

El Dia 24 de Enero de 1917 acontecicio la desgracia a la Sra. Tivurcia Gallego en el pueblo de Darginfilio Texas que llendo por la via del tren ella y un chamaquito que llebara de la mano y al ir sobre un puente los alcansaron unos trabajadores en un puchicarro con maletas y no pudiendo acerse ni para un lado ni para otro invocó la Sma. Virgen de San Juan habiendo sufrido nada mas unos golpes ella y el chamaquito nada mas sonzo del golpe habiendose librado de un peligro mayor y en accion de gracias dedica este retablo.

(COLECCIÓN DURAND-ARIAS)

The misfortune happened to Mrs. Tivurcia Gallego on the 24th day of January 1917, in the town of Daingerfield, Texas. She was walking along a train track holding a little boy by the hand, and as she went over a bridge, some workers with trunks overtook them in a pushcar. Being unable to move to either side, she invoked the Holiest Virgin of San Juan and suffered nothing more than a few blows, and the little boy no more than a glancing blow, having freed himself from greater danger. In thanksgiving she dedicates this retablo.

El dia 21 de Enero de 1917 Acontecicio la desgracia a la
Sra. Tivurcia Gallego en el pueblo de Darginfilio Texas que
Llendo por la via del tren ella y un chamaquito que llebabadela
mano y al ir sobre un puente los alcansaron unos trabajadores
en un puchicarro con maletas y no pudiendo acerse ni para un
lado ni para otro invoco a la Sma. Virgen de San Juan
habiendo sufrido nada mas unos golpes ella y el chamaquito nada
mas sonzo del golpe habiendose librado de un peligro mayor
y en accion de gracias dedica este retablo.

Figure 1
Retablo of Tivurcia Gallego.
1917. Oil on metal. 20.3 × 15.3 cm.
Durand-Arias collection.

Retablo of Juan Luna

▼▼▼

El día 15 de enero de 1942 habiéndome disgustado con mis compañeros con quienes fuí a trabajar al estado de Tamaulipas me separé de ellos internándome en un bosque fuí a dar a una casa donde pedi permiso y como a las diez de la noche el dueño de la casa me llamó fuera tratándome de bandido me dijo que me iba a matar por lo que viendome en tan grave peligro me encomende a la Santísima Virgen de Sn. Juan de los Lagos y a Sn. Martín de Terreros. Juan Luna.

(COLECCIÓN DURAND-ARIAS)

On the 15th day of January of 1942, after becoming annoyed with my companions with whom I went to work in the state of Tamaulipas, I separated from them. Advancing deeply into a woods, I went up to a house to ask permission, and since it was ten at night the owner of the house called me outside and mistook me for a bandit. He said that he was going to kill me, and seeing myself in such grave danger I entrusted myself to the Holiest Virgin of San Juan de los Lagos and to St. Martin of Terreros. Juan Luna.

El dia 15 de enero de 1947 habiéndome dis gustado con mis com- pañeros con quienes fui a trabajar al estado de Tamaulipas

me separé de ellos internán- dome en un bosque fui a dar a una casa donde pe- dí permiso y como a las diez de la noche el dueño de la casa me llamó fuera tratándome de bandido me dijo que me iba a matar por lo que viendome en tan grave peligro me encomende a la Santisima Virgen de Sn Juan de los Lagos y a Sn Martin de Terreros. Juan Luna

Figure 2
Retablo of Juan Luna.
1942. Oil on metal. 18.2 × 25.6 cm.
Durand-Arias collection.

Retablo of José Cruz Soria

▼▼▼

Doy infinitas gracias a Nuestra Sra. de Sn. Juan de los Lagos por haber podido pasar la frontera y por regresar con salud. José Cruz Soria. San Miguel de Allende, Gto. Febrero 2–1960.

(COLECCIÓN DURAND-ARIAS)

I give infinite thanks to Our Lady of San Juan de los Lagos for having enabled me to cross the border and return with health. José Cruz Soria. San Miguel de Allende, Guanajuato. February 2, 1960.

Figure 3
Retablo of José Cruz Soria.
1960. Oil on metal. 17.2 × 18 cm.
Durand-Arias collection.

Retablo of Amador de Lira

Amador de Lira le da las mas infinitas grasias por el milagro de avelos livrado al pasar el peligroso rio en Texas.

(COLECCIÓN DURAND-ARIAS)

Amador de Lira gives the most infinite thanks for the miracle of saving them as they crossed the dangerous river in Texas.

Figure 4
Retablo of Amador de Lira.
Undated. Oil on metal. 14.7 × 24.4 cm.
Durand-Arias collection.

Retablo of Domingo Segura

▼▼▼

El 28 de Mayo 1929 me sucedio la desgracia de haver sido arrastrado por las aguas del Rio Vravo (en El Paso-Texas) y viéndome en tan gran peligro invoque con veras de mi corazón a Ntra. Sra. de San Juan de los Lagos y al momento acudio a mi salvasión un compañero mio el cual luchando con denuedo las temerosas aguas logró sacarme salvo al margen del río y en acción de gracias por tan patente milagro hago público el precente retablo. San Francisco del Rincón. Enero 29 de 1932. Domingo Segura.

(SANTUARIO DE SAN JUAN DE LOS LAGOS)

The misfortune happened to me on May 28, 1929. Being dragged along by the waters of the Rio Grande in El Paso, Texas, I saw myself in such great danger that I invoked Our Lady of San Juan de los Lagos with a true heart, and at that moment my salvation came from a friend who, bravely fighting the fearful waters, was able to pull me to the river bank. In thanksgiving for so apparent a miracle, I make public the present retablo. San Francisco del Rincón. January 29 of 1932. Domingo Segura.

El 28 DE Mayo DE 1919 ME SUCEDIO LA DESGRACIA DE HAVER SIDO ARRASTRADO POR LAS AGUAS DEL RIO VRAVO (EN EL PASO-TEXAS) Y VIENDOME EN TAN GRAN PELIGRO INVOQUE CON VERAS DE MI CORAZON A Nᵃ Sᵃ DE SAN JUAN DE LOS LAGOS. Y AL MOMENTO ACUDIO A MI SALVASION UN COMPAÑERO MIO EL CUAL LUCHANDO CON DENUEDO LAS TEMEROSAS AGUAS LOGRO SACARME SALVO AL MARGEN DEL RIO Y EN ACCION DE GRACIAS POR TAN PATENTE MILAGRO HAGO PUBLICO EL PRECENTE RETABLO.
SAN FRANCISCO DEL RINCON.
ENERO 27 DE 1932.
Domingo Segura.

Figure 5
Retablo of Domingo Segura.
1932. Oil on metal. Dimensions unknown.
Sanctuary of San Juan de los Lagos.

Retablo of Braulio Barrientos

▼▼▼

Rcho. Palencia. Sn. Diego de la Unión, Gto.
11 Enero de 1986. Con esta fecha dedico
este retablo a la Virgen de Sn. Juan por tan
patente milagro que nos consedió ya que con
fecha 5 de Junio de 1986 al remigrar a E.U.
con 3 compañeros se nos terminó el agua que
llevamos siendo me el camino con el fuerte
calor y la sed sin esperanzas de tomar un
poco de agua. Invocamos a la Sma. Virgen
de San Juan de los Lagos y logramos llegar
a nuestro destino y regresar a nuestra patria
con salud. En eterno agradecimiento desde el
lugar donde se encuentre Braulio Barrientos a
la Sma. Virgen de Sn. Juan de los Lagos Jal.

(SANTUARIO DE SAN JUAN DE LOS LAGOS)

Rancho Palencia, San Diego de la Unión,
Guanajuato. January 11, 1986. On this date
I dedicate the present retablo to the Virgin of
San Juan for the clear miracle she granted on
the date of June 5, 1986. Re-emigrating to the
United States with three friends, the water we
were carrying ran out. Traveling in such great
heat and with such thirst, and without hope
of drinking even a little water, we invoked the
Virgin of San Juan and were able to arrive at
our destination and return to our homeland in
health. In eternal gratitude to the Virgin of
San Juan de los Lagos from the place where
you find Braulio Barrientos.

Figure 6

Retablo of Braulio Barrientos.

1986. Oil on metal. Dimensions unknown.

Sanctuary of San Juan de los Lagos.

Retablo of M. Esther Tapia Picón

Damos gracias a la virjen de San Juan por librarnos de los de la migración al pasar a Los Anjeles. León, Gto. M. Esther Tapia Picón.

(SANTUARIO DE SAN JUAN DE LOS LAGOS)

We give thanks to the Virgin of San Juan for saving us from the migration authorities on our way to Los Angeles. León, Guanajuato. María Esther Tapia Picón.

DAMOS GRACIAS A LA VIRJEN DE SAN
JUAN POR LIBRARNOS DE LOS DE LA
MIGRACION AL PASAR A LOS ANJELES
LEON GTO M. ESTHER TAPIA PICON

Figure 7
Retablo of M. Esther Tapia Picón.
Undated. Oil on metal. Dimensions unknown.
Sanctuary of San Juan de los Lagos.

Retablo of Concepción Zapata

Dedico el presente RETABLO a la Sma. V. de
San Juan de los Lagos por aberme salbado
de un TEXANO me llebara, me escodi debajo
de un arbol con mi hermanito ala orilla de la
carretera. Concepcion Zapata. S.L.P. Mayo 10
de 1948.

(COLECCIÓN DURAND-ARIAS)

I dedicate the present retablo to the Holiest
Virgin of San Juan de los Lagos for having
saved me from a Texan who tried to carry me
off. I hid under a tree by the side of the road
with my little brother. Concepción Zapata.
San Luis Potosí. May 10, 1948.

Figure 8

Retablo of Concepción Zapata.

1948. Oil on metal. 14 × 19.5 cm.

Durand-Arias collection.

Retablo of Elifonsa Durán

▼▼▼

La Señorita M. Elifonsa Durán se fue a los Estados Unidos del Norte y al saver su mamá que estaba muy delicado se la encomendo a la Virgen de San Juan que si no la molestaban y que regresara con vien le daba gracias en este retablo.

Miss María Elifonsa Durán went to the United States, and when her mother found out that she was very delicate she commended her to the Virgin of San Juan, saying that if they didn't bother her and that if she returned with well-being, she would give her thanks in this retablo.

LA SEÑORITA M. ELIFONSA DURÁN
SE FUE A LOS ESTADOS UNIDOS DEL NORTE Y
AL SAVER SU MAMÁ QUE ESTABA MUY
DELICADO SE LA ENCOMENDO A LA VIRGEN
DE SAN JUAN QUE SINO LA MOLESTABAN
Y QUE REGRESARA CON VIEN LE DABA GRA —
CIAS EN ESTE RETABLO.

Figure 9
Retablo of Elifonsa Durán.
Undated. Oil on metal. 24.3 × 17.5 cm.
Durand-Arias collection.

Retablo of Isidro Rosas Rivera
▼▼▼

*Madre mia de San Juan de los Lagos te
doy infinitas grasias por el milagro que me
consediste por aberme orientado y guiado acia
el Rancho Brackiville, Tex. sin yo saber por
tal motibo Virgencita Milagrosa ago patente
el milagro y dedico este retablo. Isidro Rosas
Rivera. Rancho Hda. de Jesus. Municipio Sn.
Luis de la Paz, Gto. Año 1976.*

(COLECCIÓN DURAND-ARIAS)

My Mother of San Juan de los Lagos, I give
you infinite thanks for the miracle that you
granted, without me knowing it, of guiding
me to the ranch in Brackettville, Texas.
For this reason, Miraculous Little Virgin,
I make apparent the miracle and dedicate
this retablo. Isidro Rosas Rivera. Rancho
Hacienda de Jesús. Municipio San Luis de la
Paz, Guanajuato. Year 1976.

Madre mia de San Juan de los Lagos te doy infinitas
Grasias por el Milagro que me consediste Por aberme
Orientado y guiado a cia el Rancho. Brackiville. Tex. sin
Yo saber. Por tal motibo Virgencita Milagrosa ago
Parente el Milagro Ydedico este Retablo.
Isidro Rosas Rivera Rancho Hda. de Jesus. Municipio,
Sn. Luis de la Paz Gto.   Año. 1976.

Figure 10
Retablo of Isidro Rosas Rivera.
1976. Oil on metal. 18 x 24.8 cm
Durand-Arias collection.

Retablo of Matías Lara

18 De Nobiembre 1919 encontrondome yo
perdido en chicago me encomende a La Virgen
de San Juan de los Lagos pidiendole que
me iluminara al camino que buscaba y doy
gracias por aberme consedido. lo que yo le
pedi por eso le dedico el presente retablo como
un recuerdo. Matias Lara. San Luis Potosi.

(COLECCIÓN MASSEY-ROSS)

On November 18, 1919, finding myself lost
in Chicago I entrusted myself to the Virgin
of San Juan de los Lagos, asking that she
illuminate the road that I sought. I give her
thanks for granting me what I asked, and for
this reason dedicate the present retablo as a
memento. Matías Lara. San Luis Potosí.

18. De Nobienbre de 1918 encontrandome Yo perdido en chicago
Me encomiendo a la Virgen de San Juan de Los Lagos pidiedoleo que
me iluminara al Camino que buscaba y doy gracias por Aberme Cons
cdido lo que Yo le pedi por Eso le Dedico el presente Retablo Como
Un Recuerdo Matias Lara San Luis Potosi

Figure 11
Retablo of Matías Lara.
1919. Oil on metal. 30.5 × 20.3 cm.
Massey-Ross collection.

Retablo of Juan Sánchez R

Con el presente retablo le pido al Sr de la Conquista su intersección para solucionar un problema para arreglar unos papeles de importancia de E.U.A. JUAN SANCHEZ R. San Felipe, Gto. Nobre 20—1990.

(SANTUARIO DEL SEÑOR DE LA CONQUISTA)

With the present retablo I request the intercession of the Lord of the Conquest to resolve a problem of arranging some papers of importance in the U.S.A. JUAN SANCHEZ R. San Felipe, Guanajuato, November 20—1990.

Con el presente retablo le pido al Sr de la Conquista, su intersección para --
solucionar un problema para arreglar unos papeles de importancia de E.U.A.

JUAN SANCHEZ R.

San Felipe, Gto

Nobre 20 - 1990

Figure 12
Retablo of Juan Sánchez R.
1990. Oil on metal. Dimensions unknown.
Sanctuary of Our Lord of the Conquest.

Retablo of Victoriano Grimaldo

Doy infinitas gracias a la Santísima virgen de "San Juan" por haber concedido el milagro de salir de prisión en E.E.U.U., encontrándonos mi tío, mi primo, y Yo, en agradecimiento dedico el presente. Feb./88. San Felipe, Gto. Victoriano Grimaldo.

(COLECCIÓN DURAND-ARIAS)

I give infinite thanks to the Holiest Virgin of San Juan for granting me the miracle of leaving prison in the U.S.A. along with my uncle and cousin. In thanksgiving I dedicate the present retablo. February 1988. San Felipe, Guanajuato. Victoriano Grimaldo.

Doy infinitas gracias a la Santísima virgen de "San Juan" por - haber concedido el milagro, de salir de prisión en E.E.U.U., encontrándonos mi tío, mi prima y Yo, en agradecimiento dedico el presente. Feb./88. San Felipe, Gto.   Victoriano Grimaldo.

Figure 13
Retablo of Victoriano Grimaldo.
1988. Oil on metal. 25 × 30 cm.
Durand-Arias collection.

Retablo of Juan Jose Sánches O

Con el presente retablo le pido al Sr. de la Conquista Que permita que me den mi Libertad en Estados Unidos. San Felipe, Gto. Juan Jose Sánches O. Oct. 10 de 1990.

(SANCTUARIO DEL SEÑOR DE LA CONQUISTA)

With the present retablo I ask the Lord of the Conquest that he allow them to give me my liberty in the United States. San Felipe, Guanajuato. Juan José Sánchez O. October 10, 1990.

Con el presente retablo le pido al Sr. de la Conquista
Que permita que me den mi libertad en Estados Unidos.

SAN FELIPE GTO.   Juan Jose Sánches C.   Oct. 10 de 1990.

Figure 14
Retablo of Juan Jose Sánches O.
1990. Oil on metal. Size unknown.
Sanctuary of Our Lord of the Conquest.

Retablo of unknown votary

Estando detenido . . . Sierra Rica con unos Texanos [   ] a mi la autoridadad americana me castigó severamente y yo me perdí esperanzas de salir. Inboqué a Nuestra Señora de San Juan de los Lagos y hago patente el milagro [   ].

(COLECCIÓN DURAND-ARIAS)

Being detained in Sierra Rica with some Texans [   ] to me. The American authorities punished me severely and I lost hope of leaving. I invoked Our Lady of San Juan de los Lagos and I make apparent the miracle [   ].

Figure 15

Retablo of unknown votary.

Undated. Oil on metal. 25.8 × 36 cm.

Durand-Arias collection.

Retablo of Bernabé H. and Catarina V

▼▼▼

Encontrándome muy malo de unos calam-
bres estube por días en un sanatorio de
NAURASKA, E.U. por lo que encontrándome
en tan triste situcíon invoqué al Sr. del
SAUCITO, la Virgen de Guadalupe, y ala
Virgen de S. Juan para que me dieran salud.
Bernavé H. Catarina V. 7-4-1944.

(COLECCIÓN DURAND-ARIAS)

Finding myself suffering from bad cramps
I was confined for days in a sanatorium in
Nebraska, U.S.A. Being in such a sad state,
I invoked the Lord of Saucito, the Virgin
of Guadalupe, and the Virgin of San Juan
that they should give me health. Bernabé H.
Catarina V. 7-4-1944.

ENCONTRÁNDOME MUY MALO DE UNOS ALAMBRES ESTUBE POR
DÍAS EN UN SANATORIO DE NAURASKA. E.U. POR LO QUE ENCO
EN TAN TRISTE SITUCIÓN IMBOQUÉ AL SR DEL SAUCITO, LA VIRGE
GUADALUPE Y A LA VIRGEN DE S. JOHN PARA QUE ME DIERA N AC
BERNAVE H. CATARINA V.   H 7-4-1944.

Figure 16
Retablo of Bernabé H. and Catarina V.
1944. Oil on metal. 18 × 25.8 cm.
Durand-Arias collection.

Retablo of Paula Martínez

Dedíco el precente retablo a La Sma. Virgen de San Juan de los Lagos. en acción de gracias por el milagro que me hizo consediéndonos la salud a mi nieta María Silvia Arevalo y a mí, que nos encontrábamos gravemente enfermas. Paula Martínez. Dona, Texas, E.U.A. Marzo de 1964.

(COLECCIÓN DURAND-ARIAS)

I dedicate the present retablo to the Holiest Virgin of San Juan de los Lagos in thanksgiving for the miracle she granted me. She gave health to me and my granddaughter, María Silvia Arévalo, when we found ourselves gravely ill. Paula Martínez. Donna, Texas, U.S.A. March of 1964.

Figure 17
Retablo of Paula Martínez.
1964. Oil on metal. 24 × 18.6 cm.
Durand-Arias collection.

Retablo of Dolores R. García

▼▼▼

Gracias a la Virgen de San Juan de los Lagos por haberle vuelta su salud a mi nieto Phillip M. García en el año de 1964 de parte de su abuelita Dolores R. García en este día 27 de Agosto 1968. Kingsburg, Calif. U.S.A.

(COLECCIÓN DURAND-ARIAS)

Thanks to the Virgin of San Juan de los Lagos for having returned health to my grandson, Phillip M. García, in the year 1964, from his grandmother, Dolores R. García, on this 27th day of August, 1968. Kingsburg, California, U.S.A.

Figure 18
Retablo of Dolores R. García.
1968. Oil on metal. 25.4 × 35.6 cm.
Durand-Arias collection.

Retablo of Venancio Soriano

Venancio Soriano—Estando trabajando en Harlingen, Texas, contrajo una grave enfermedad en el pulmón izquierdo, que se creía incurable, ofreciendo a la milagrosa Virgencita de San Juan de los Lagos, visitarla y traerle el presente como una muestra de gratitud por su alivio.

(COLECCIÓN DURAND-ARIAS)

Venancio Soriano. While at work in Harlingen, Texas, I contracted a grave illness of the left lung that was thought incurable. I offered to visit the Miraculous Little Virgin of San Juan de los Lagos and bring her this retablo as proof of gratitude for her relief.

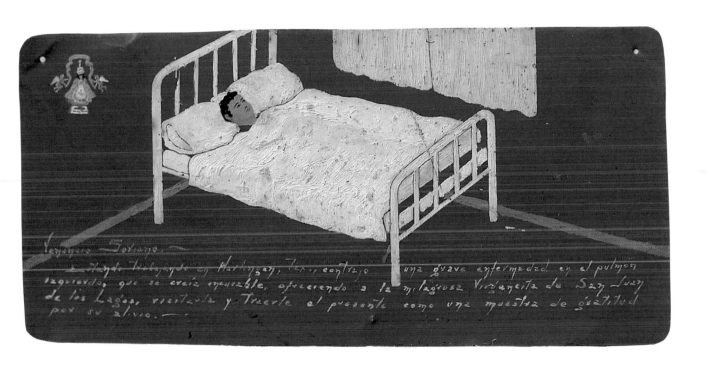

Figure 19
Retablo of Venancio Soriano.
Undated. Oil on metal. 15 × 31 cm.
Durand-Arias collection.

Retablo of Eulalia Ortiz

*Eulalia Ortiz Da gracias al Señor de Villaseca
por haberse recuperado de su enfermedad.
Desde Modesto California.*

(SANTUARIO DE VILLASECA)

Eulalia Ortiz gives thanks to our Lord of
Villaseca for having recovered from her
sickness. From Modesto, California.

Figure 20
Retablo of Eulalia Ortiz.
Undated. Oil on metal. Dimensions unknown.
Sanctuary of Villaseca.

Retablo of María de la Luz Casillas and Children
▼▼▼

Doy Gracias a la Sma. Virgen de Sn. Juan de los Lagos por aberme Echo el Milagro tan Grande de Salvarme de Una Peligrosa Operación que me fue Echa por Segunda Vez, El día 9 de Octubre de 1960, en los Angeles, California. La cual me puso a las Puertas de la Muerte y Encomendada a tan Milagrosa Virgen pude Recobrar mi Salud. por la cual Ago patente El presente Retablo: En señal de Agradecimiento Dando Gracias a la Santísima Virgen de San Juan. Los Angeles Cal. Agosto de 1961. María de la Luz Casillas e hijos.

(COLECCIÓN DURAND-ARIAS)

I give thanks to the Holiest Virgin of San Juan de los Lagos for having made me so great a miracle of saving me in a dangerous operation that was performed on me for the second time on the 9th day of October 1960, in Los Angeles, California. Which put me at the doors of death but entrusted to so miraculous a Virgin I could recover my health, for which I make apparent the present retablo: in sign of thanksgiving I give thanks to the Holiest Virgin of San Juan. Los Angeles, California. August 1961. María de la Luz Casillas and children.

Doy Gracias a la Sma. Virgen de Sn. Juan de los lagos por aberme Echo el Milagro tan Grande de Salvarme de una Peligrosa Operacion que me fue Echa por Segunda Vez, El dia 9 de Octubre de 1960 en los Angeles California la cual me puso alas Puertas de La Muerte y Encomendada a tan Milagrosa Virgen pude Recobrar mi Salud. por la cual, ago Patente El presente Retablo: En señal de Agra decimiento Dando Gracias ala Sma. Virgen de Sn Juan ·(((Los Angeles Cal. Agosto de 1961.)))··

Maria de la Luz Casillas. e hijos.

Figure 21
Retablo of María de la Luz Casillas and Children.
1961. Oil on metal. 17.3 × 26 cm.
Durand-Arias collection.

Retablo of Antonia Ramos de González
▼▼▼

Doy infinitas gracias a la Santísima Vir-gen de S. Juan pues me concedió mi salud en una operación muy peligrosa. Gracias madre mía. Antonia Ramos de Glez. Oxnar Calif.-Mayo-9-1971.

(COLECCIÓN DURAND-ARIAS)

I give infinite thanks to the Holiest Virgin of San Juan because she conceded me my health in a very dangerous operation. Thank you my Mother. Antonia Ramos de González. Oxnard, California. May 9, 1971.

Doy Infinitas Gracias a la Santisima Virgen de S. Juan pues me concedio mi salud en una operacion muy peligrosa. GRACIAS MADRE MIA.

Antonia Ramos de Glez.
Oxnar Calif-mayo-9-1971.

Figure 22
Retablo of Antonia Ramos de González.
1971. Oil on metal. 20 × 32.2 cm.
Durand-Arias collection.

Retablo of Consuelo and Juanita de León
▼▼▼

Angel Ortíz. Estimado hijo: Sabiendo que mi hijo se encontraba muy grave en los Estados Unidos en el hospital, ahí lo tenían con cadenas amarrado a una cama porque corría, lo amarraban de los pies y de los brazos, mirando eso aclamé a la Santícima Virgen de San Juan de los Lagos y la Virgen de Guadalupe de México, D.F. para que le dieran su alivio. Le dedican este retablo su mamá la Sra. Consuelo de León y su hermana Juanita de León. a 13 de Mayo de 1988.

(SANTUARIO DE SAN JUAN DE LOS LAGOS)

Angel Ortiz. Esteemed son: Learning that my son was very ill in a hospital in the United States, and that they had chained him to a bed because he tried to run away, and that they had bound him by the feet and arms, I invoked the Holiest Virgin of San Juan de los Lagos and the Virgin of Guadalupe in Mexico, D.F., to give him relief. His mother, Mrs. Consuelo de León, and her sister, Juanita de León, dedicate this retablo to [them]. May 13, 1988.

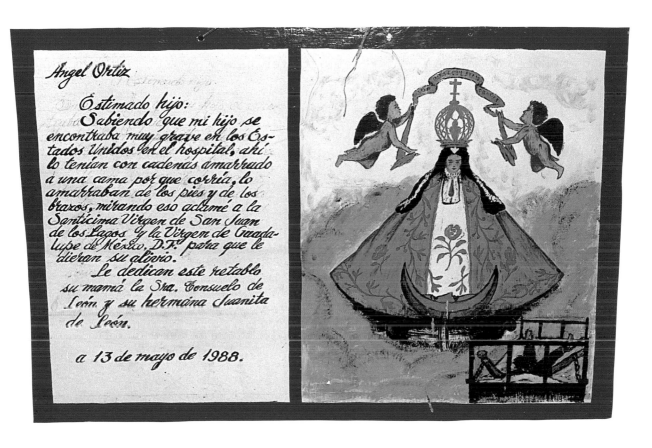

Angel Ortiz

Estimado hijo:
Sabiendo que mi hijo se
encontraba muy grave en los Estados Unidos en el hospital, ahí
lo tenían con cadenas amarrado
a una cama por que corría, lo
amarraban de los pies y de los
brazos, mirando eso aclamé a la
Santícima Virgen de San Juan
de los Lagos y la Virgen de Guadalupe de México, D.F. para que le
dieran su alivio.
Le dedican este retablo
su mamá la Sra. Consuelo de
León y su hermana Juanita
de León.

a 13 de mayo de 1988.

Figure 23
Retablo of Consuelo and Juanita de León.
1988. Oil on metal. Dimensions unknown.
Sanctuary of San Juan de los Lagos.

Retablo of Juanita Limón

Doy gracias al Señor de la Misericordia por haber librado a mi esposo de ir a la Guerra a Corea. Juanita Limón. Needles, California. Enero 24, 1956. U.S.A.

(SANTUARIO DEL SEÑOR
DE LA MISERICORDIA)

I give thanks to the Lord of Mercy for having freed my husband from going to the war in Korea. Juanita Limón. Needles, California. January 24, 1956. U.S.A.

Figure 24

Retablo of Juanita Limón.

1956. Oil on metal. Dimensions unknown.

Sanctuary of the Lord of Mercy.

Retablo of Paula Vázquez de F

Doy gracias a el Santo Niño de Atocha por haberme concedido el milagro. Paula Vázquez de F. Viet Nam.

(SANTUARIO DEL NIÑO DE ATOCHA)

I give thanks to the Holy Child of Atocha for having granted me the miracle. Paula Vázquez de F. Vietnam.

DOY GRACIAS A EL
SANTO NIÑO DE
ANTOCHA
POR HABERME CONCEDIDO
EL MILAGRO

PAULA VAZQUEZ DE F.

Figure 25
Retablo of Paula Vázquez de F.
Undated. Oil on metal. Dimensions unknown.
Sanctuary of the Child of Atocha.

Retablo of Gumercindo Ramírez
▼▼▼

El día 5 de Abril de 1908, a Gumercindo Ramirez, en Florences, Kansas, E.U.A. se cayó de la carrucha pasando por encima de él quebrándole las costillas y dejándolo bien muerto. Pero antes de esto se encomendó a la M. S. de S. Juan quien lo libró y en prueba del maravilloso milagro dedico el presente recuerdo. S. Francisco del Rincón. Febrero 2 de 1912.

(COLECCIÓN DURAND-ARIAS)

On the 5th day of April of 1908, Gumercindo Ramírez fell from a handcar in Florence, Kansas, U.S.A. It ran over him and broke his ribs, leaving him near death. But as he fell he entrusted himself to the Miraculous Lady of San Juan who saved him, and in proof of this marvelous miracle I dedicate the present memento. San Francisco del Rincón. February 2, 1912.

Figure 26
Retablo of Gumercindo Ramírez.
1912. Oil on metal. 18 × 25.7 cm.
Durand-Arias collection.

Retablo of Marciano Alcocer Castillo
▼▼▼

Voto de Gratitud a la "Stma. Virgen de San Juan" Me accidenté y quedé lastimado de la cintura y perdí de trabajar y la aseguranza no me reconocía mi enfermedad para que me pagara lo que me correspondía. Me encomendé a la Stma. Virgen de San Juan, y me hizo el milagro, me alivió y me llegó el cheque correspondiente de mi accidente. Marciano Alcocer Castillo dedica éste Retablo a la Virgen de San Juan en agradecimiento. Matehuala, S.L.P. Mayo 16 de 1967.

(COLECCIÓN DURAND-ARIAS)

Votive of gratitude to the Holiest Virgin of San Juan. I had an accident and was injured in the lower back and couldn't work. The insurance company wouldn't recognize my injury and pay what they owed me, so I commended myself to the Holiest Virgin of San Juan, and she gave me the miracle. She made me get better and sent me the check from my accident. Marciano Alcocer Castillo dedicates this retablo to the Virgin of San Juan in thanks. Matehuala, San Luis Potosí. May 16, 1967.

Figure 27
Retablo of Marciano Alcocer Castillo.
1967. Oil on metal. 24.7 × 31.3.
Durand-Arias collection.

Retablo of Senovio Trejo

Encontrándome en Estados Unidos trabajando en el algodón y al transportarnos de un lado a otro se nos desconpuso el carro chocando en un poste de la luz. El cual me pegó en el serebro viéndome en tan grande peligro lejos de mi patria y de mi familia. Me encomendé de todo mi corazón a San Miguelito. León, Gto. Senovio Trejo.

(CAPILLA DE SAN MIGUEL)

While in the United States working in the cotton fields, I was moving from place to place when the car broke down and crashed into a light post. It struck me on the head and put me in very great danger far from my homeland and my family. I entrusted myself with all my heart to San Miguelito. León, Guanajuato. Senovio Trejo.

ENCONTRANDOME EN ESTADOS UNIDOS TRABAJANDO EN EL ALGODON Y AL TRASPORTARNOS DE UN LADO A OTRO SE NOS DES CONPUSO EL CARRO CHOCANDO EN UN POSTE DE LA LUZ EL CUAL ME PEGO EN EL SEREBRO VIENDOME EN TAN GRANDE PELIGRO Y LEJOS DE MI PATRIA Y DE MI FAMILIA ME ENCOMENDE DE TODO MI CORAZON A Sr SAN MIGUELITO. LEON GTO. SENOVIO TREJO

Figure 28
Retablo of Senovio Trejo.
Undated. Oil on metal. Dimensions unknown.
Chapel of Saint Michael.

Retablo of Manuela Sánchez and Children
▼▼▼

Ago precente este milagro, llendo mi hijo y su esposa por una carretera del Paso de Texas en una curva dio 3 bueltas y quedando sin centido y sin esperanza de vida y la ciencia medica no se encontro capas y lo encomendé a la Virgen Sma. de San Juan a las 12 horas bolvio en si sin la menor dolencia del golpe hoy damos gracias yo Manuela Sánchez y mis hijos Manuel y Elena. Febrero 28 de 1947. Accidentado en Abril de 1934.

(COLECCIÓN MASSEY-ROSS)

I make apparent this miracle. As my son and his wife were traveling on a highway near El Paso, Texas, they did three flips while going around a turn, which left him senseless and without hope of life. Because medical science found itself incapable of healing him, I entrusted him to the Holiest Virgin of San Juan and after 12 hours he came to without the slightest pain from the blow. Manuela Sánchez and her children, Manuel and Elena, today give thanks. February 28, 1947. The accident occurred in April of 1934.

Figure 29
Retablo of Manuela Sánchez and Children.
1947. Oil on metal. 22 × 14.5 cm.
Massey-Ross collection.

Retablo of Angela Chávez

Damos grasias a la Santísima Virgen de San Juan de los Lagos de librarme de una enfermedad grave a consecuencia de un choke que peresí. Angela Chávez. Los Angeles California. 1940.

(SANTUARIO DE SAN JUAN DE LOS LAGOS)

I give thanks to the Holiest Virgin of San Juan de los Lagos for saving me from a grave illness because of a crash that I nearly died in. Angela Chávez. Los Angeles, California. 1940.

DAMOS GRASIAS A LA SANTISIMA. VIRGEN DE SAN JUAN DE LOS LAGOS DE LIBRARME DE UNA
ENFERMEDAD GRAVE ACONSECUENSIA DE UN CHOKE QUE PERESI ANJELA. CHAVEZ.
LOS ANJELES CALIFORNIA 1940

Figure 30
Retablo of Angela Chávez.
1940. Oil on metal. Dimensions unknown.
Sanctuary of San Juan de los Lagos.

Retablo of Jesús Domingo Herrera
▼▼▼

Jesus Domingo Herrera del pueblo 2 de Abril, Municipio de Guadalupe Victoria Durango, Dgo. da infinitas gracias a la Sma. Virgen de San Juan de los Lagos por Librarme de un accidente automovilístico que me sucedió en el Lugar de Massing, Idaho, de Estados Unidos. Al prestar mis servicios como bracero. Siendo asi, caminaba yo por la carretera cuando un automovil me atopelló arrojandome a 20 mts. de distancia quedando sin sentido. Restablecido pago mi manda. El accidente me sucedió el día 14 de Mayo de 1946.

(SANTUARIO DE SAN JUAN DE LOS LAGOS)

Jesús Domingo Herrera, from the town "April Second" in the Municipio of Guadalupe Victoria, Durango, gives infinite thanks to the Holiest Virgin of San Juan de los Lagos for freeing him from an automobile accident that happened in Marsing, Idaho, the United States. Offering my services as a bracero, I was walking along a highway when an automobile struck me and dragged me a distance of 20 meters, leaving me senseless. Restored, I pay my debt. The accident happened to me on the 14th day of May 1946.

Jesús Dominguez Herrera, del Pueblo 2 de Abril Municipio de Guadalupe Victoria Durango. Dgo. da infinitas gracias a la Sma. Virgen de "San Juan de los Lagos" por Librarme de un accidente automovilistico que me sucedió en el Lugar de Massura, Idaho, de Estados Unidos. Al prestar mis servicios como bracero, siendo así, caminaba ya por la carretera cuando un automovil me atropelló arojandome a 20 mts. de distancia quedando sin sentido. Restableciedo pago mi manda... El accidente me sucedió el dia 14 de Mayo de 1946...

Figure 31
Retablo of Jesús Domingo Herrera.
1946. Oil on metal. Dimensions unknown.
Sanctuary of San Juan de los Lagos.

Retablo of Josefina Rivera

La Señorita Josefina Rivera da Infinitas
Gracias a la Sma. Virgen de Sn. Juan de los
Lagos por salvarle la Vida al Caer Bajo las
Ruedas de un Camion. Brownsville, Texas.
Agosto 25 1954.

(COLECCIÓN DURAND-ARIAS)

Miss Josefina Rivera gives infinite thanks to
the Holiest Virgin of San Juan de los Lagos for
saving her life after falling beneath the wheels
of a bus. Brownsville, Texas. August 25,
1954.

La Señorita Josefina Rivera da Infinitas Gracias a la Sma
Virgen de Sn. Juan de los lagos por Salvarle la Vida al Caer
Bajo las Ruedas de un Camion Brownsville Texas Agosto 25 1954

Figure 32
Retablo of Josefina Rivera.
1954. Oil on metal. 22.2 × 30 cm.
Durand-Arias collection.

Retablo of J. Cruz Ontiveros
▼▼▼

Doy gracias al Sr. San Miguelito porque me hizo el milagro de que saliera con bien de un accidente que tuve con una camioneta en una carretera en Wajanachie, Texas, U.S.A. En agradecimiento le dedico el presente. San Felipe, Gto. 16 Septiembre 1972. J. Cruz Ontiveros.

(CAPILLA DE SAN MIGUEL)

I give thanks to the Lord Saint Michael for granting me the miracle of coming out well from an accident that I had in a pickup truck on the highway in Waxahachie, Texas, U.S.A. In thanks I dedicate the present retablo. San Felipe, Guanajuato. September 16, 1972 J. Cruz Ontiveros.

Figure 33
Retablo of J. Cruz Ontiveros.
1972. Oil on metal. Dimensions unknown.
Chapel of St. Michael.

Retablo of Jesús Gómez G

Doy gracias al Señor de la Misericordia por
un favor resivido. Julio del 81. Compton, Cal.
Jesus Gomez G.

(SANTUARIO DEL SEÑOR

DE LA MISERICORDIA)

I give thanks to the Lord of Mercy for a favor
received. July 1981. Compton, California.
Jesús Gómez G.

Figure 34
Retablo of Jesús Gómez G.
1981. Oil on metal. Dimensions unknown.
Sanctuary of the Lord of Mercy.

Retablo of Antonio Alcaraz
▼▼▼

Doy infinitas gracias a la Santísima Vírgen de San Juán de los Lagos. Por aberme concedido el volver con vida al lado de mi familia. Después de un terrible acontesimiento al regresar a mi Pueblo. Venía yo de los estados Unidos Americanos, cuando después de haber cruzada la frontera al encontrarme en el estado Chihuahua fuí asaltado en el trén que nos conducía a nuestros hogares. Por unos ladrones que querian privarme de la vida para robarme el dinero y cuanto yo traia. Pero no lograron su intento gracias a la Sma. Virgen, cuando un ladron me tira con el puñal me hize el impulso a defenderme con tan fuerza que rompi con mi espalda el cristal de la ventanilla por donde fui a da asia afuera cayendo al suelo tan fuerte que sufre que por nada pierdo la vida. Y como si esto no fuese suficien se volco la camioneta en que fuí recogido para condusirme al hospital. Este acontesimiento fue el 20 de noviembre de 1943 a las 7 de la noche. Antonio Alcaraz. Zacapu, Mich. 2-2-49.

(SANTUARIO DE SAN JUAN DE LOS LAGOS)

I give infinite thanks to the Holiest Virgin of San Juan de los Lagos for allowing me to return alive to my family's side after a terrible event that occurred during my return to town. I was coming from the United States of America when, just after crossing the border in Chihuahua, I was assaulted on the train by thieves who wanted to take my life and rob me of the money and all that I carried. But they didn't accomplish their goal thanks to the Holiest Virgin. When the bandit struck at me with a dagger, an impulse made me defend myself with such force that I broke a glass window with my back and fell backwards outside, landing on the ground so hard that I thought for sure I would lose my life. And if this was not enough, the van that picked me up to bring me to the hospital turned over. This happened on November 20, 1943 at 7:00 in the evening. Antonio Alcaraz. Zacapu, Michoacán. 2-2-49.

Doy infinitas gracias a la Santísima Virgen de San Juan de los Lagos.
Por haberme concedido el volver con vida al lado de mi familia.
Después de un terrible acontesimiento, al regresar a mi
Pueblo. Venía yo de los estados Unidos Americanos, cuando después
da haber cruzado la frontera al encontrarme en el estado Chihuahua
Fui asaltado en el crén que nos conducía a nuestros hogares.
Por unos ladrones que querían privarme de la vida para robarme
el dinero y cuanto yo traía.
Pero no lograron su intento, gacias a la Sma Virgen. cuando un ladron
me tira con un puñal hize el impulso a defenderme tan Fuerte que rompí
con mi espalda el cristal de la ventanilla por donde Fui a da osia a Fuera
cayendo al suelo tan Fuerte que por nada pierdo la vida.
y como si esto no fuese suficien se volco la camioneta en
que Fui recogido para condusirme al hospital.
este acontesimiento fue el 20 de noviembre de 1943
a las 7 de la noche. Antonio Alcaraz
Zacapu Mich. 2-2-44

Figure 35
Retablo of Antonio Alcaraz.
1949. Oil on metal. Dimensions unknown.
Sanctuary of San Juan de los Lagos.

Retablo of Candelaria Arreola

Doy gracias a la Sma. Virgen de Talpa por haberme traído a mi hijo de Estados Unidos que duró mucho tiempo, empecé a resar su noven(a) y aun no le terminaba cuando regresó. ¡Gracias madre mía! El Grullo, Jal. 1955 Candelaria Arreola.

(COLECCIÓN DURAND-ARIAS)

I give thanks to the Holiest Virgin of Talpa for having brought my son home from the United States, where he stayed for a long time. I began to pray your novena and I hadn't even finished when he returned. Thank you, my Mother! El Grullo, Jalisco, 1955. Candelaria Arreola.

DOY GRACIAS ALA SMA. VIRGEN DE TALPA POR HABERME TRAIDO A MI
HIJO DE LOS ESTADOS UNIDOS QUE DURO MUCHO TIEMPO, EMPECE A REGAR
SU NOVEN Y AUN NO LA TERMINABA CUANDO REGRESO.
¡GRACIAS MADRE MIA!
EL GRULLO, JAL. 1955   CANDELARIA ARREOLA.

Figure 36
Retablo of Candelaria Arreola.
1955. Oil on metal. 24 × 17.5 cm.
Durand-Arias collection.

Retablo of Francisco Trujillo

*Doy muchísimas gracias al Sr. de los Milagros
porque encomendados a El un hijo logró sanar
de un fuerte dolor que padecía en el estómago
y el otro hijo apareció después de tener un
tiempo perdido con todo mi agradecimiento
hago patente este milagro dedicándole este
retablo. Varal Norte, Mpio. San Felipe, Gto.
Noviembre 8 de 1976. Francisco Trujillo.*

(COLECCIÓN DURAND-ARIAS)

I give thanks to the Lord of Miracles because,
entrusted to him, one son was cured of a
strong pain that he suffered in the stomach
and the other son reappeared after being
lost for some time. With all my thankfulness
I make apparent this miracle, dedicating
to him this retablo. Varal Norte, Municipio
San Felipe, Guanajuato. November 8, 1976.
Francisco Trujillo.

Doy muchisimas gracias al Sr. de los milagros porque encomenda
dos a El, un hijo logró sanar de un fuerte dolor que padecia en el estóma
go y el otro hijo apareció, después de tener un tiempo perdido, con to
do mi agradecimiento, hago patente este milagro dedicandole este retabl
Varal Norte, mpio. San Felipe, Gto. noviembre 8 de 1976.   Francisca Trujillo.—

Figure 37
Retablo of Francisco Trujillo.
1976. Oil on metal. 25 × 19.5 cm.
Durand-Arias collection.

Retablo of María Marcos Rebolloso and Leonardo Arsola
▼▼▼

Doy infinitas gracias al Sr. de los Milagros
porque encomendado a El, sanó mi hijo
Leonardo Arsola, de una enfermedad muy
desconocida que tenía, y porque espero, que
regresen otros 3 hijos, que están en E.U. uno
con su familia y los otros 2 solteros. San
Felipe, Gto. 4 de Julio 1977. María Marcos
Rebolloso. Leonardo Arsola.

(COLECCIÓN DURAND-ARIAS)

I give infinite thanks to the Lord of Miracles
because, entrusted to him, he healed my son
Leonardo Arsola, from an unknown sickness.
I also hope for the return of my other three
sons who are in the U.S., one with his family
and the other two bachelors. San Felipe,
Guanajuato, July 4, 1977. María Marcos
Rebolloso. Leonardo Arsola.

Doy infinitas gracias al Sr. de los milagros, porque encomendado a El, sano mi hijo Leonardo Arsola, de una enfermedad muy desconocida que tenia, y porque espero, que regresen otros 3 hijos, que estan en E.U. uno con su familia y las otros 2 solteros.

María Marcos Rebolloso

San Felipe, Gto. 4 de Julio/1977.   Leonardo Arsola

Figure 38
Retablo of María Marcos Rebolloso and Leonardo Arsola.
1977. Oil on metal. 25 × 18.5 cm.
Durand-Arias collection.

Retablo of F.P. from El Coesillo, San Luis Potosí
▼▼▼

Doy Gracias a Dios y al Señor de los Milgros por Haberme Hecho El Milagro Que mi Hijo Regresara Del Norte Haviendo Arreglado Sus papeles. Por Lo Que Doy Gracias a Dios y Dedico este Recuerdo al Señor de los Milagros. F. P. el Coesillo, San Felipe, Gto.

(COLECCIÓN DURAND-ARIAS)

I give thanks to God and the Lord of Miracles for having granted me the miracle of allowing my son to return from el norte after arranging his papers. For this I give thanks and dedicate this memento to the Lord of Miracles. F. P. El Coesillo, San Felipe, Guanajuato.

Doy GraCIas a Dios y al Señor DeLos MILaGro Por Haber
me Hecho El MILaGro Que mi Hijo ReGresara Del monTe
HavIenDo ArreGLaDo Sus PaPeles. Por lo Que
Doy GraTIas a Dios y DeDICo esTe RecuerDo al
Señor De Los MiLaGros. F. P.   el Coesillo San felipe Gto

Figure 39
Retablo of F.P. from El Coesillo, San Luis Potosí.
Undated. Oil on metal. 18.5 × 15.5 cm.
Durand-Arias collection.

Retablo of Carmen Ortíz

La-Sra. *"Carmen-Ortiz" en-comendó-a-la-Virgen-de-San. Juan-de-los-Lagos. -a-su-esposo. Sr. Mateo Hernández, que-regresara-de los Estados-Unidos. -Y-se en-contrava-en-fermo-de-la vista lo-cual-dan-gracias. por-su-favor. "Núñez."*

(COLECCIÓN DURAND-ARIAS)

Mrs. Carmen Ortiz commended her husband, Mr. Mateo Hernández, to the Virgin of San Juan de los Lagos, that he should return from the United States after he found himself sick in his eyes. For this they give thanks for her favor. "Núñez."

RETABLO.

MILAGRO
C.O.

M.H.

LA-SRA. "CARMEN-ORTIZ" EN-COMENDO-A-
LA-VIRGEN-de-SAN. JUAN-de-LOS-LAGOS. A-
SU-ESPOSO. SR. MATEO HERNANDEZ, QUE-
REGRESARA-de-LOS ESTADOS-UNIDOS. Y-SE
EN-CONTRAVA-EN-FERMO-de-LA-VISTA
LO-CUAL-DAN-GRACIAS. POR-SU-FAVOR

Figure 40
Retablo of Carmen Ortíz.
Undated. Oil on metal. 25.5 × 18 cm.
Durand-Arias collection.

References
▼▼▼

Aceves Barajas, Pascual. 1956. *Hermenegildo Bustos: Su vida y su obra*. Guanajuato, Guanajuato: Imprenta Universitaria.

Almanza Carranza, Ezequiel. 1981. *Relatos y sucedidos de Guanajuato*. León, Guanajuato: Talleres Lino-tipográficos Lumen, S.A.

Alvarez, José Rogelio. 1987. *Enciclopedia de México*. Vol. 12. México, D.F.: Secretaría de Educación Pública y Enciclopedia de México.

Amado, Jorge. 1966. *Bahía de Todos os Santos*. Sao Paulo: Livraria Martins Editora.

Archivo Histórico de Jalisco. 1906. E S 1906, Jalisco, 115.

Archivo Histórico de la Ciudad de León, Guanajuato. 1910. "Expediente sobre inmigración." 31 de Mayo.

Aspiazu, José María. 1991. Interview by Héctor Hernández with Father Jose Maria Aspiazu, Founding Priest, Shrine of San Juan del Valle, August 1991, San Antonio, Texas.

Atl, Dr. (Gerardo Murillo). 1922. *Las artes populares en México*. Vol. 2. México, D.F.: Editorial Cultura y la Secretaría de Industria y Comercio.

Baker, Carlos. 1969. *Ernest Hemingway: A Life Story*. New York: Charles Scribner's Sons.

Baker, Mark. 1981. *Nam: The Vietnam War in the Words of the Men and Women Who Fought There*. New York: William Morrow & Co.

Bartel, Ann. 1989. "Where Do the New U.S. Immigrants Live?" *Journal of Labor Economics* 7:371–91.

Bean, Frank D., and Marta Tienda. 1987. *The Hispanic Population of the United States*. New York: Russell Sage.

Benítez, Fernando. 1965. *The Century After Cortés*. Chicago: University of Chicago Press.

Berdecio, Robert, and Stanley Appelbaum. 1972. *Posada's Popular Mexican Prints*. New York: Dover Publications.

Bowman, Russell. 1985. "Martín Ramírez: A Visionary's Journey." In *The Heart of Creation: The Art of Martín Ramírez*, 16–27. Philadelphia: Moore College of Art.

Cardinal, Roger. 1986. "El mensaje de Martín Ramírez." *Vuelta* 10(112):56–58.

Cardoso, Lawrence. 1980. *Mexican Emigration to the United States 1897 1931*. Tucson: The University of Arizona Press.

Carrillo Dueñas, Manuel. 1986. *Historia de Nuestra Señora del Rosario de Talpa*. México, D.F.: Impresos Alfa.

Carrillo y Gariel, Abelardo. 1949. *Técnica de las Esculturas en Caña*. México, D.F.: Dirección General de Monumentos Coloniales.

Casa de Cultura. 1991. *Tres siglos de pintura religiosa en San Luis Potosí*. México, D.F.: Secretaría de Educación Pública.

Casillas, Luis Alberto. 1989. *Apuntes para la Historia del Señor de la Misericordia*. Tepatitlán, Jalisco: Editorial Privado.

Charlot, Jean. 1963. *The Mexican Mural Renaissance, 1920–1925*. New Haven, Conn.: Yale University Press.

————. 1949. "Mexican Ex-Votos." *Magazine of Art* 42:139–42.

Conover, Ted. 1987. *Coyotes: A Journey Through the Secret World of America's Illegal Aliens*. New York: Vintage.

Cornelius, Wayne A. 1976. "Outmigration from Rural Mexican Communities." *Interdisciplinary Communications Program Occasional Monograph Series* 5(2):1–39.

Cousin, Bernard. 1982. *Le Miracle et le Quotidien: Les Ex-votos Provençaux, Images d'une Société*. Paris: Sociétés, Metalités, et Cultures.

Craig, Richard B. 1971. *The Bracero Program: Interest Groups and Foreign Policy*. Austin: University of Texas Press.

Creux, René. 1979. *Les Ex-Voto Racontent*. Geneva: Editions de Fontainnemore.

Dagodag, W. Tim. 1975. "Source Regions and Composition of Illegal Mexican Immigration to California." *International Migration Review* 9:499–511.

Decouflé, Pierre. 1964. "La Notion d'Ex-Voto Anatomique chez les Etrusco-Romains." *Latomus, Revue d'Etudes Latines* 72:5–41.

de la Maza, Francisco. 1950. "Los retablos dorados de Nueva España." *Enciclopedia Mexicana del Arte*. México, D.F.: Ediciones Mexicanas.

Díaz de León, Francisco. 1985. *Gahona y Posada, grabadores mexicanos*. México, D.F.: Fondo de Cultura Económica.

Donato, Katharine M., Jorge Durand, and Douglas S. Massey. 1992. "Stemming the Tide? Assessing the Deterrent Effects of the Immigration Reform and Control Act." *Demography* 29:139–57.

Durand, Jorge. 1991. *Migrations Internationales dans l'ouest du Mexique: Conditions Sociales, Politques et Culturelles*. Ph.D. diss., New Program in Geography and Urbanism, University of Toulouse.

Durand, Jorge, and Douglas S. Massey. 1990. *Doy Gracias: Iconografía de la Emigración México-Estados Unidos*. Guadalajara, Jalisco: Programa de Estudios Jaliscienses, Secretaría de Educación Pública, Universidad de Guadalajara, e Instituto Nacional de Antropología e Historia.

————. 1992. "Mexican Migration to the United States: A Critical Review." *Latin American Research Review* 27:3–42.

Egan, Martha. 1991. *Milagros: Votive Offerings from the Americas*. Santa Fe: Museum of New Mexico Press.

Escobedo, Helen. 1989. *Mexican Monuments: Strange Encounters*. New York: Abbeville Press.

Espenshade, Thomas J. 1990. "Undocumented Migration to the United States: Evidence from a Repeated Trials Model." In *Undocumented Migration to the United States: IRCA and the Experience of the 1980s*, edited by Frank D. Bean, Barry Edmonston, and Jeffrey Passel, 159–81. Washington, D.C.: The Urban Institute.

Fernández, Celestino. 1983. "The Mexican Immigration Experience and the Corrido Mexicano." *Journal of Studies in Latin American Popular Culture* 2:115–30.

Fernández, Celestino, and James E. Officer. 1989. "The Lighter Side of Mexican Immigration: Humor and Satire in the Mexican Corrido." *Journal of the Southwest* 31(4):471–96.

Fernández, Justino. 1952. *Arte moderno y contemporáneo de México*. México, D.F.: Imprenta Universitaria.

Fernández, Miguel Angel. 1983. *Obras maestras de la pintura en los museos de México*. México, D.F.: Planeta.

Fussell, Paul. 1975. *The Great War and Modern Memory*. New York: Oxford University Press.

Galarza, Ernest. 1964. *Merchants of Labor: The Mexican Bracero Story*. Santa Barbara, Calif.: McNally and Loftin.

Gamio, Manuel. 1930. *Mexican Immigration to the United States*. Chicago: University of Chicago Press.

———. 1931. *The Mexican Immigrant: His Life Story*. Chicago: University of Chicago Press.

Garduño Pulido, Blanca. 1990. "Diego Rivera y Frida Kahlo en el rescate de los retablos mexicanos." In *Milagros en la frontera: Los mojados de la Virgen de San Juan dan gracias por su favor*, edited by Blanca Garduño Pulido, Carolina Sada, and María Eugenia López Saldaña, 7–10. México, D.F.: Consejo Nacional para la Cultura y las Artes y el Instituto Nacional de Bellas Artes.

Garduño Pulido, Blanca, Carolina Sada, and María Eugenia López Saldaña, eds. 1990. *Milagros en la frontera: Los mojados de la Virgen de San Juan dan gracias por su favor*. México, D.F.: Consejo Nacional para la Cultura y las Artes y el Instituto Nacional de Bellas Artes.

Genaro Cuadriello, Jaime. 1989. *Maravilla americana: Variantes de la iconografía guadalupana*. Guadalajara: Patrimonio Cultural del Occidente.

Giffords, Gloria K. 1974. *Mexican Folk Retablos: Masterpieces on Tin*. Tucson: The University of Arizona Press.

———. 1991. "The Art of Private Devotion: Retablo Painting of Mexico." In the catalog to the exhibition The Art of Private Devotion: Retablo Painting of Mexico, 33–63. Dallas-Fort Worth: InterCultura and the Meadows Museum.

Goldring, Luin P. 1992. "Gendered Memory: Reconstructions of the Village by Mexican Transnational Migrants." Paper presented at the 8th World Congress of Rural Sociology, University Park, Penn., August 11–16.

González, Jorge. 1986. "Exvotos y retablitos: Religión popular y comunicación social en México." *Estudios sobre culturas contemporáneas* 1(1):7–51.

Griffith, James S. 1987. "El Tiradito and San Juan Soldado: Two Victim-Intercessors of the Western Borderlands." *International Folklore Review* 5:75–81.

———. 1992. *Beliefs and Holy Places: A Spiritual Geography of the Pimería Alta*. Tucson: The University of Arizona Press.

Hansen, Roger D. 1971. *The Politics of Mexican Development.* Baltimore: Johns Hopkins University Press.

Hart, John M. 1987. *Revolutionary Mexico: The Coming and Process of the Mexican Revolution.* Berkeley: University of California Press.

Herr, Michael. 1978. *Dispatches.* New York: Avon Books. "Emigración de mexicanos." 1907. *Heraldo de Zamora*, 11 de agosto, Zamora, Michoacán.

Herrera, Hayden. 1983. *Frida: A Biography of Frida Kahlo.* New York: Harper and Row.

Herrera-Sobek, María. 1979. *The Bracero Experience: Elitelore vs. Folklore.* Washington, D.C.: UCLA Latin American Center.

Hondagneu-Sotelo, Pierette. 1992. "Overcoming Patriarchal Constraints: The Reconstruction of Gender Relations Among Mexican Immigrant Women and Men." *Gender and Society* 6:393–415.

Jakovsky, Anatole. 1949. "The Ex-Votos of Notre-Dame de Laghet." *Magazine of Art* 42(4):143–45.

Jasso, Guillermina, and Mark R. Rosenzweig. 1990. *The New Chosen People: Immigrants in the United States.* New York: Russell Sage.

Jones, Richard D. 1981. "Channelization of Undocumented Mexican Migrants to the United States." *Economic Geography* 58:156–76.

Juárez Frías, Fernando. 1991. *Retablos populares mexicanos: Iconografía religiosa del siglo XIX.* México, D.F.: Inversora Bursátil, S.A.

Knight, Alan. 1986. *The Mexican Revolution.* Cambridge: Cambridge University Press.

Kossoudji, Sherrie A. 1992. "Playing Cat and Mouse at the U.S.-Mexican Border." *Demography* 29:159–80.

Lafaye, Jacques. 1976. *Quetzalcóatl and Guadalupe: The Formation of Mexican National Consciousness, 1531–1813.* Chicago: University of Chicago Press.

Longhauser, Elsa W. 1985. Foreword to *The Heart of Creation: The Art of Martin Ramirez*, 3–5. Philadelphia: Moore College of Art.

López Castro, Gustavo. 1986. *La casa dividida: Un estudio de caso sobre migración a Estados Unidos en un pueblo michoacano.* Zamora, Michoacán: El Colegio de Michoacán.

López de Lara, J. Jesús. 1991. "Plateros y el Santo Niño de Atocha." In *Retablos populares mexicanos: Iconografía religiosa del siglo XIX*, by Fernando Juárez Frías, 199–200. México, D.F.: Inversora Bursátil, S.A

———. 1992. *El Niño de Santa María de Atocha.* 4th ed. Fresnillo, Zacatecas: Santuario de Platerios.

Lowe, Sarah M. 1991. *Frida Kahlo.* New York: Universe Publishing.

Martin, Stephen. 1985. "Martín Ramírez: Psychological Hero." In *The Heart of Creation: The Art of Martin Ramirez*, 28–44. Philadelphia: Moore College of Art.

Martínez Peñaloza, Porfirio. 1988. *Arte popular y artesanías en México: Un acercamiento.* SEP Lecturas Mexicanas, Segunda Serie, No. 108. México, D.F.: Secretaría de Educación Pública.

Massey, Douglas S., Rafael Alarcón, Jorge Durand, and Humberto González. 1987. *Return to Aztlán: The Social Process of International Migration from Western Mexico.* Berkeley and Los Angeles: University of California Press.

Massey, Douglas S., Luin P. Goldring, and Jorge Durand. 1994. "Continuities in Transnational Migration: An Analysis of 19 Communities." *American Journal of Sociology* 99:1492–1533.

McGonigle, Thomas. 1985. "Violated Privacy: Prose for Martín Ramírez." *Arts* 55:155–57.

Metropolitan Museum of Art. 1990. *Mexico: Splendors of Thirty Centuries.* Boston: Little, Brown, and Company.

Meyer, Jean A. 1976. *The Cristero Rebellion: The Mexican People Between Church and State, 1926–1929.* New York: Cambridge University Press.

Mines, Richard. 1981. *Developing a Community Tradition of Migration: A Field Study in Rural Zacatecas, Mexico, and California Settlement Areas.* Monographs in U.S.-Mexican Studies No. 3. La Jolla, Calif.: Program in United States Mexican Studies, University of California San Diego.

Montenegro, Roberto. 1934. *Pintura mexicana 1800–1860/Mexican Painting 1800 1860.* México, D.F.: Secretario de Educación Pública.

————. 1950. *Retablos de México/Mexican Votive Paintings.* México, D.F.: Ediciones Mexicanas.

Moyssén, Xavier. 1965. "La pintura popular y costumbrista del siglo XIX." *Artes de México* 61, Año XIII.

North, David S., and Houstoun, Marion F. 1976. *The Characteristics and Role of Illegal Aliens in the U.S. Labor Market: An Exploratory Study.* Washington, D.C.: Linton.

Oblate Fathers. 1991. "A Short History of the Virgin of San Juan del Valle Shrine." Pamphlet. San Juan, Tex.: Oblate Fathers.

Oettinger, Marion, Jr. 1991. Foreword to *Milagros: Votive Offerings from the Americas*, by Martha Egan, vi–ix. Santa Fe: Museum of New Mexico Press.

Olveda, Jaime. 1980. "La Feria de San Juan de los Lagos." *El Informador.* Guadalajara, September 7.

Orendain, Leopoldo. 1948. "Exvotos." In *Cuarto Centenario de la Fundación del Obispado de Guadalajara. 1548 1948*, 279–90. Guadalajara: Artes Gráficas.

Palais Lascaris. 1987. *Ex-Voto et Penitents.* Nice: Palais Lascaris, Musée des Arts et Traditions Populaires.

Paz, Octavio. 1961. *The Labyrinth of Solitude: Life and Thought in Mexico.* New York: Grove Press.

————. 1988. "Yo pintor, indio de este pueblo." *Vuelta* 10(113):35–50.

Pérez, Peter. 1991. Interview by Héctor Hernández with Father Peter Pérez, Chief Priest at the Shrine of San Juan del Valle, San Juan, Texas, August 1991.

Polanco Brito, Hugo. 1984. *Exvotos y "Milagros" del Santuario de Higuey.* Santo Domingo, Dom. Rep.: Ediciones del Banco Central.

Posada, José Guadalupe. 1930. *Posada Monografía.* México, D.F.: Talleres Gráficos de la Nación.

Ramírez, Fausto. 1990. "The Nineteenth Century." In the catalog to the exposition *Mexico: Splendors of Thirty Centuries*, 499 538. New York: Metropolitan Museum of Art.

Ramos, Samuel. 1962. *Profile of Man and Culture in Mexico.* Austin: University of Texas Press.

Ranney, Susan, and Sherrie Kossoudji. 1983. "Profiles of Temporary Mexican Labor Migrants to the United States." *Population and Development Review* 9:475–93.

Reavis, Dick J. 1992. *Conversations with Moctezuma: The Soul of Modern Mexico.* New York: William Morrow.

Redfield, Robert. 1930. *Tepoztlán: A Mexican Village.* Chicago: University of Chicago Press.

Reichert, Joshua S. 1979. *The Migrant Syndrome: An Analysis of U.S. Migration and its Impact on a Rural Mexican Town.* Ph.D. diss., Department of Anthropology, Princeton University.

———. 1982. "A Town Divided: Economic Stratification and Social Relations in a Mexican Migrant Community." *Social Problems* 29:411–23.

Reyna, Elba. 1991. Interview by Héctor Hernández with Elba Reyna, Chief of Personnel, Shrine of San Juan del Valle, San Juan, Texas, August 1991.

Rivera, Diego. 1958. *José Guadalupe Posada: Artista popular*. México, D.F.: Artes de México.

———. 1979. *Arte y Política*. México, D.F.: Editorial Grijalbo.

Romandía de Cantú, Graciela. 1978. *Exvotos y milagros mexicanos*. México, D.F.: Compañía Cerillera la Central.

Ruy Sánchez, Alberto. 1992. "Hermenegildo Bustos: Pintor del gesto comunitario." In *Hermenegildo Bustos: Ex-votos*. México, D.F.: Fundación Cultural Cremi.

Salazar, María. 1991. Interview by Héctor Hernández with Señora María Salazar, Secretary of Information, Shrine of San Juan del Valle, San Juan, Texas, August 1991.

Samora, Julian. 1971. *Los mojados: The Wetback Story*. Notre Dame: University of Notre Dame Press.

Sánchez, Apolinar. 1991. Interview by Héctor Hernández with Apolinar Sánchez, Sacristan of the Church of San Juan del Valle, San Juan, Texas, August 1991.

Sánchez Lara, Rosa María. 1990. *Los retablos populares: exvotos pintados*. México, D.F.: Universidad Nacional Autónoma de México, Instituto de Investigaciones Estéticas.

Sandoval Godoy, Luis. 1984. *Reina de Jalisco: Historia y costumbrismo en torno a la imagen de Nuestra Señora de Zapopán*. Guadalajara: Talleres Fotolitográficos de Impresores.

Santoli, Al. 1981. *Everything We Had: An Oral History of the Vietnam War by Thirty-Three American Soldiers Who Fought It*. New York: Random House.

Schroeder, Francisco Arturo. 1968. "Plateresco." *Retablos mexicanos: Artes de México* 106, Año XV.

Siems, Larry, ed. 1992. *Between the Lines: Letters Between Undocumented Mexican and Central American Immigrants and their Families and Friends*. Hopewell, N.J.: The Ecco Press.

Siqueiros, David Alfaro. 1977. *Me llamaba el coronelazo*. México, D.F.: Editorial Grijalbo.

Smith, Roberta. 1985. "Radiant Space: The Art of Martín Ramírez." In *The Heart of Creation: The Art of Martin Ramirez*, 6–15. Philadelphia: Moore College of Art.

Solís, Felipe. 1991. *Tesoros artísticos del Museo Nacional de Antropología*. México, D.F.: Editorial Aguilar.

Sordo, Emma María. 1990. "Del Cajón San Marcos al retablo testimonio." *Cuadernos de Arte y Cultura Popular* 1:9–14.

Steele, Thomas J. 1982. *Santos and Saints: The Religious Folk Art of Hispanic New Mexico*. Santa Fe: Ancient City Press.

Taylor, Paul. 1932. "Mexican Labor in the United States: Chicago and the Calumet Region." In *University of California Publications in Economics*, edited by Carl C. Plehn, Ira B. Cross, and Melvin M. Knight, vol. 7, no. 2, 25–284. Berkeley: University of California Press.

———. 1933. "A Spanish-Mexican Peasant Community: Arandas in Jalisco, Mexico." *Ibero-American*. Vol 4. Berkeley: University of California Press.

———. 1935. "Songs of the Mexican Migration." In *Puro Mexicano*, edited by J. Frank Dobie, 221–45. Texas Folk-Lore Society Publications Number XII. Austin: Texas Folk-Lore Society.

Tibol, Raquel. 1983. *Hermenegildo Bustos: Pintor del pueblo.* Guanajuato: Gobierno del Estado de Guanajuato.

———. 1986. *Diego Rivera: Ilustrador.* Mexico, D.F.: Secretaría de Educación Pública.

Toor, Frances. 1947. *A Treasury of Mexican Folkways.* New York: Crown Publishers.

Townsend, Richard F., ed. 1992. *The Ancient Americas: Art from Sacred Landscapes.* Munich: Prestel Verlag.

Urrea, Luis Alberto. 1993. *Across the Wire: Life and Hard Times on the Mexican Border.* New York: Ancho.

U.S. Bureau of the Census. 1991. *The Hispanic Population of the United States: March 1991.* Current Population Reports, Series P-20, No. 455. Washington, D.C.: U.S. Government Printing Office.

U.S. Immigration and Naturalization Service. 1992. *1991 Statistical Yearbook of the Immigration and Naturalization Service.* Washington, D.C.: U.S. Government Printing Office

Valle Arizpe, Artemio. 1941. "El exvoto." *Notas de Platería.* México, D.F.: Editorial Polis.

Vasconcelos, José. 1926. "The Race Problem in Latin America." In *Aspects of Mexican Civilization*, edited by José Vasconcelos and Manuel Gamio, 75–104. Chicago: University of Chicago Press.

Vidal, Teodoro. 1972. *Los milagros en metal y en cera de Puerto Rico.* San Juan: Ediciones Alba.

Villezcas, Bernadina. 1991. Interview by Héctor Hernández with Bernadina Villezcas, Original Promotor of the Shrine of San Juan del Valle, San Juan, Texas, August 1991.

Villezcas, Jesús. 1991. Interview by Héctor Hernández with Jesús Villezcas, Son of Original Promotor of the Shrine of San Juan del Valle, San Juan, Texas, August 1991.

Westheim, Paul. 1951. *Hermenegildo Bustos: Catálago de la Exposición.* México, D.F.: Museo Nacional de Artes Plásticas.

Woodrow, Karen A., and Jeffrey S. Passel. 1990. "Post-IRCA Undocumented Immigration to the United States: An Assessment Based on the June 1988 CPS." In *Undocumented Migration to the United States: IRCA and the Experience of the 1980s*, edited by Frank D. Bean, Barry Edmonston, and Jeffrey S. Passel, 33–76. Washington, D.C.: The Urban Institute.

Zamora, Martha. 1990. *Frida Kahlo: The Brush of Anguish.* San Francisco: Chronicle Books.

Index

▼▼▼

About the Authors
▼▼▼

Jorge Durand undertook his undergraduate studies at the Universidad Iboamericana in Mexico City and went on to complete graduate work in social anthropology at the Colegio de Michoacán (where he earned his M.A.) and the University of Toulouse, France (where he received his Ph.D.). He has served as Professor and Investigator at the Center for the Study of Social Movements at the Universidad de Guadalajara since 1988. He is the author of *La ciudad invade al ejido* (Ediciones Casa Chata, Mexico City, 1983), *Los obreros del Rio Grande* (El Colegio de Michoacán Press, 1986), and *Caminos de antropología* (Instituto Nacional Indígena, 1992). For more than a decade he has collaborated with Douglas Massey in studying Mexican migration to the United States, and with him he has written two books on the subject: *Return to Aztlán* (University of California Press, 1987) and *Doy gracias* (Programa de Estudios Jaliscienses, 1990). He has published several other books on international migration by himself, including *Migración México Estados Unidos: Anos veinte* (Consejo Nacional de la Cultura, 1991), *Les Lueve Sobre Mojado* (Instituto Tecnologico y de Estudios Superiores de Occidente, 1991), and most recently *Más allá de la línea* (Consejo Nacional de la Cultura, 1994).

In addition to his expertise in migration studies, Jorge Durand has long pursued interests in culture and the arts. In 1992 he helped to create a guide for the Museum of the City of Guadalajara, and he has participated in a number of expositions of popular Mexican art, including one on migrants' retablos organized by the Diego Rivera Studio-Museum. Over the years he has delivered numerous papers and lectures about the origin and diffusion of the ex-voto in Mexico.

After receiving his Ph.D. in Sociology from Princeton University, **Douglas S. Massey** undertook postdoctoral studies in demography at the University of California at Berkeley and went on to assume faculty positions at the University of Pennsylvania and the University of Chicago, where from 1991 to 1994 he directed the Center for Latin American Studies; in 1994 he returned to the University of Pennsylvania as the Dorothy Swaine Thomas Professor of Sociology. He is a past member of the Committee on Hispanic Policy Issues of the Social Science Research Council and since 1992 has served as chair of the Committee on South-North Migration of the International Union for the Scientific Study of Population.

In addition to his two books with Jorge Durand, Douglas Massey recently published, in collaboration with Nancy Denton, *American Apartheid* (Harvard University Press, 1993), a detailed study of racial segregation and its role in creating the urban underclass. He is the author of more than 60 scholarly articles, about evenly divided between the subjects of Mexican migration and racial segregation. He has testified before the U.S. Congress on several occasions on topics as varied as immigration, the North American Free Trade Agreement, the Fair Housing Act, and U.S. race relations. Like Durand, he has lectured widely before scholars and the public on Mexican retablo painting, including a presentation at the Mexican Fine Arts Museum of Chicago.